I Brake
for
Yard Sales

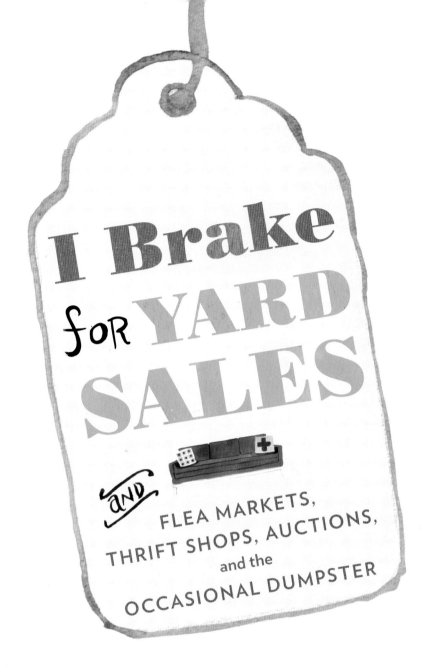

I Brake for YARD SALES

and

FLEA MARKETS,
THRIFT SHOPS, AUCTIONS,
and the
OCCASIONAL DUMPSTER

Lara Spencer

FOREWORD BY

Kathy Griffin

PHOTOGRAPHS BY MICHAEL MCNAMARA
ILLUSTRATIONS BY CAITLIN MCGAULEY

STEWART, TABORI & CHANG   NEW YORK

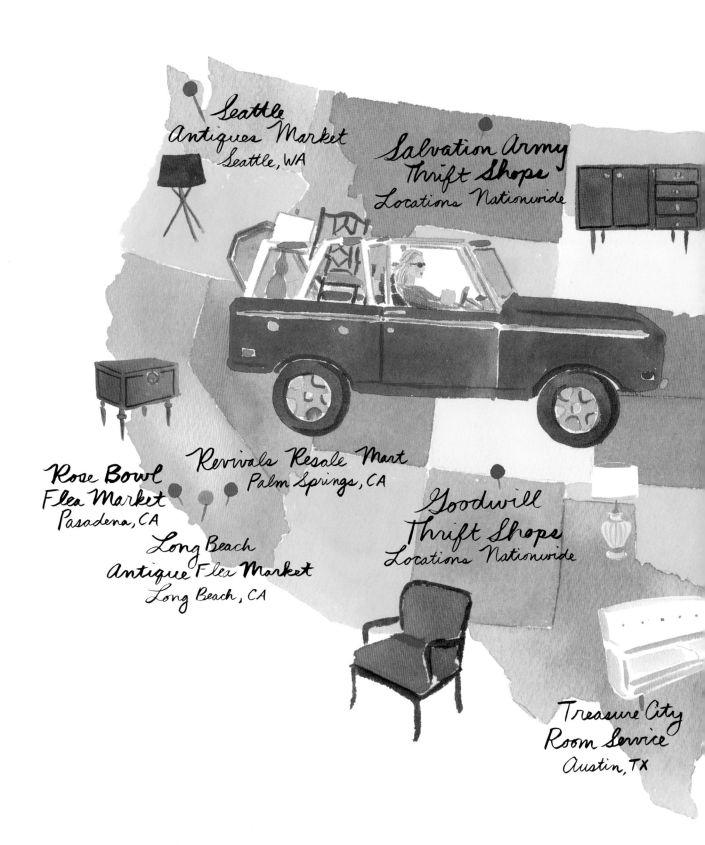

Seattle
Antiques Market
Seattle, WA

Salvation Army
Thrift Shops
Locations Nationwide

Revivals Resale Mart
Palm Springs, CA

Rose Bowl
Flea Market
Pasadena, CA

Long Beach
Antique Flea Market
Long Beach, CA

Goodwill
Thrift Shops
Locations Nationwide

Treasure City
Room Service
Austin, TX

Favorite Haunts

Brimfield
Brimfield, MA

Northeast
Auctions
Portsmouth, NH

Elephant's Trunk
New Milford, CT

Clark Auction Gallery
Larchmont, NY

Greenwich Hospital
Thrift Shop
Greenwich, CT

Housing Works
New York, NY

Brooklyn Flea
Brooklyn, NY

Brown Elephant
Resale Shops
Chicago, IL

World's Longest Yard Sale
from Michigan to Alabama

Scott's
Antique Market
Atlanta, GA

Church Mouse
Palm Beach, FL

Woman's Exchange
Thrift Shop
Sarasota, FL

Table of Contents

Foreword

BY KATHY GRIFFIN

Here I am showing Kathy and her
amazing mom, Maggie, my work
for the very first time! (Cameras
are there capturing the moment
for *Kathy Griffin: My Life on the
D-List*.) I was nervous, but they
loved it—whew!

I walked into my friend Lara's house, looked around, and said, "Can you do this to my house?" And guess what? She did it to my house and you can do it to yours. Her taste is impeccable. I'm convinced she can re-create any style—from her Connecticut colonial-antique coziness to the theme she used for my home, which we jokingly call "Palm Springs gay man going through a midlife crisis in his mid-century home who wants to attract the hottest guys to come over."

Lara makes this process . . . wait for it . . . *fun*! Yes, fun! If she can convince me to go to an estate sale when it's still dark outside, and to rummage through hidden treasures that I never would have picked out without her, then you're next. Yes, I was a swap meet/flea market virgin until Lara popped my cherry. I admit, the first time she took me to an estate sale I was convinced that I was going to get crabs or be purchasing chairs covered in old-lady urine, but we ended up just laughing about all that. The next thing I knew, Lara chose several pieces that were perfect for my house and then had them re-covered or, as we call it, "repurposed." Repurposed is my new favorite word!

While designing or remodeling your living space can be stressful or confusing, and likely to go over budget, Lara can guide you on how to bring it in on time and on budget. You will learn how to work a garage sale, an estate sale, or clearance sale like a pro. I didn't have to wait sixteen weeks for a chair to be reupholstered or a footstool to be in stock. Oh no, the Spencer style is all about repurposing, researching online, and then combining those treasures and finds with a few new items that aren't on the sale rack so you'll get a mixture of one-of-a-kind pieces and the latest trend in light fixtures or flooring. When you're redesigning anything from a small powder room to your entire house, you need someone with a good eye, and that's what Lara has.

I learned so much from her. She taught me how to take an idea I saw in a design magazine and find a way to make it happen locally. Lara would find furniture that I like simply based on conversations we had where I gave a vague idea of the type of furniture I responded to. We didn't get anything from overseas nor did we overpay. The whole process was truly a fun adventure. Let this book guide you, and know that you are in good hands with Lara.

Kathy Griffin

Introduction:
To the
Bargain Born

So there I was, on a beautiful fall day in 2009, thrilled to have the house I had just completed for my family photographed for the front page of the *Los Angeles Times* Home section. It was going really well; the writer and photographer were walking from room to room, *oohing* and *aahing*, and just really loving the decor.

As we wrapped up the shoot, the writer said, "This must have cost a fortune." It was a statement, but she was definitely curious to hear the details, and I know there were a couple of ways I could have handled it.

A true blue blood would, of course, never discuss money. That would be beneath her. I, on the other hand, couldn't help myself! I dragged that poor woman around the house and described—piece by piece—what flea market, yard sale, or Dumpster I had found each piece in and what I did to fix it up. My publicist was probably mortified, but I could not have been more proud.

Welcome to my double life. All glammed up interviewing A-list celebs on a red carpet one Sunday, and getting down and dirty at a flea market the next.

I love my career in television and have been at it for a long time. I have worked in local news in Chattanooga, Tennessee, and New York, and on *Antiques Roadshow*, *The Insider*, and *Good Morning America*. I have also been moonlighting as a decorator and antiques business owner for almost a decade. What my close friends and family have known for a long time is that when the cameras stop rolling, there's nothing I would rather be doing than "sale-ing" with my kids.

Our Los Angeles home: An eclectic mix of mid-century modern, found treasures, and revamped thrift shop finds. In the master bedroom, every piece is unique, but there's a common thread in the colors.

$40

$45

$75

I wasn't kidding about the sticker.

The vintage Bronco; an eBay find!

TOP LEFT: Shopping for accessories at the Rose Bowl Flea Market in Pasadena, California.

LEFT: Occasionally the stars align and my two passions intersect, as they did when I hosted two magical seasons of the PBS classic, *Antiques Roadshow.*

That spelling is intentional. We're not talking about the water sport. Nope, no boat needed here. Just a car with a lot of storage space.

It started when I was very young. On Saturday mornings, my mom would pack me and whichever of my four older siblings she could wrangle into the family truck to navigate the sea of local yard sales.

The title of this book comes from the bumper sticker on the back of that truck. It read, I BRAKE FOR YARD SALES. That was an understatement. Full disclosure: It should have also listed illegal U-turns because Mom did her fair share of those, too. "Sale-ing," as she called it, was a cherished ritual, and in some cases, depending on the crowd, a contact sport.

The Origins of Originality

We were raised in Long Island, New York, in a beautiful town called Garden City. The stately old houses made for some great yard sale picking, as we say in the biz (the junk biz, that is), but my mom had actually never gone sale-ing until she was married. She had grown up in one of those pretty homes, elegantly appointed with antiques and art. However, when it came time to decorate her own home, she didn't have quite the same budget as her parents. With five kids to feed and my dad working his tail off, if she was going to establish that same cozy, pretty feel, she was going to have to get creative.

She was never embarrassed to be seen at a secondhand shop or yard sale. In fact, with every great find she made, she became more convinced that pulling off a great interior while being thrifty was actually very chic.

I still remember being perplexed by Mom's purchase of a beaten-up dining table at the local St. Vincent de Paul thrift shop and the smell of the stripping solution in our garage as she transformed it into a Thanksgiving dinner-worthy showpiece. It was anything but a turkey, with its shiny mahogany and

The von Seelen family. No relation to the von Trapps, but does it get WASPier than this? Knowing Mom though, the oil painting over the fireplace was from a yard sale.

That's me.

elegantly carved pedestal legs. It was blue-blood style to the core, and all it took to bring it back to its classic glory was a good eye, $68, and a little elbow grease. She taught me what I hope to pass on to you: how to see beyond frightening finishes and stained fabric, and reimagine a seemingly tired secondhand find in a modern context.

The Three Rs

It's all about the following three words: rescue, recycle, reinvent. I feel blessed that I can occasionally splurge at antique and design stores, and I sometimes do. But putting the three Rs to use is where my heart is. It's creative, it's thrifty, and it's chic. Your found treasures will add personality to your home and ensure total one-of-a-kindness. Think of it this way: Those gorgeous homes of the society set are usually filled with heirlooms, which are, at the end of the day, secondhand (or third- or fourthhand . . .) furniture.

Moving and Grooving

My day job in television brought my family to Los Angeles from the East Coast in 2008, and I was surprised to discover that my East and West Coast styles could not be more different. The common threads in our very different homes? They both reflect our family and the way we live, and both were created using the three Rs. I definitely have a split personality when it comes to design, but as you are about to see, blue-blood style is not unique to one era or look—it's about the way you put it all together.

RIGHT: Here I am in training for many future Sundays of pushing a collapsible flea market cart.

LEFT: Bonus—Treasure hunting can be a very effective workout. Forget the barbells—I'll take the barstools!

Greenwich, Connecticut
PREPPY WITH A MODERN TWIST

My friend, decorator Barclay Fryery, helped edit my many collections to give our 1920s home a warm, clubby feeling. Layering my antiques and flea market finds with pieces upholstered in leather and mohair created a cozy, layered look.

Just because you want a classic look, or want to use nineteenth-century American antiques doesn't mean you need to re-create your own colonial Williamsburg. Barclay used to tease me that all I needed was a powdered wig and a hoop skirt with all of my mahogany chests and uncomfortable chairs. He taught me that great design is about balance— mixing old and new, perfect and imperfect.

A 1940s split-reed sofa I rescued from a yard sale.

ABOVE AND RIGHT: My husband, David, and I on the front porch of our 1920s Connecticut house: gray with a wood shingle roof and a shiny black front door.

OPPOSITE: Different styles can work beautifully together, as long as you create a common thread. In my Connecticut living room, a French desk, a folk art cigar store figure, an English wing chair, and a zebra-skin rug work well to create a tailored, clubby feel.

$150

This Champagne bucket found at a yard sale does double duty as a trophy-inspired planter.

$10

Remember this?

We added the "floating" round staircase and fire pit to complement the shape of the pool. Remember the split reed sofa from our Connecticut front porch? The Trina Turk outdoor fabric takes it from safe to sexy!

Beverly Hills

HOLLYWOOD GLAM MEETS SPACE-AGE CHIC

Most of the pieces in our Connecticut house felt too traditional for our Los Angeles home. Yay! A shopportunity!

I looked for cool, one-of-a-kind finds that would help create a glamorous mid-century vibe to complement the 1961 architecture, but the airy, open floor plan meant no room for clutter. This meant fewer treasures needed—not easy for a thrifting maniac like me.

When my husband David, a real estate agent, found our West Coast house, we could tell it had great bones. They were just hiding under bad wood paneling and mauve wall-to-wall carpet. The view was blocked by heavy draperies, and there was a caged parrot with a potty mouth living in the entryway.

In a head-to-toe makeover, we opened up the dreary floor plan by getting rid of the walls on either side of the fireplace. I chose the cool gray-and-white palette to go with the house's original terrazzo floors. We replaced the wall-to-wall carpet with gray-pickled bamboo flooring. The pops of color were inspired by a vintage painting (see right) I found for next to nothing.

Yes, it's quicker and easier to order an entire room from a catalog, but where's the fun in that? For the same amount of money, or even less, I will show you how to create rooms that have a story to tell. You will find yourself taking great pride in each piece's sordid past, how much—or how little—you paid, and how you were able to give it new life. It's the ultimate Pygmalion story! The thrift shop duckling becomes your home's stylish swan, and you're creating your own family heirlooms in the process!

LEFT: Our groove-tastic Los Angeles home. We left the bones intact, including the original figure-eight pool. The giant yellow terra-cotta pots were a yard sale steal at $20 a piece.

BELOW: In its former life, the 1960s Lucite and chrome coffee table was just a topless base at a junk shop. I paid $50 for it, and another $50 for an oval piece of glass. The rug was a splurge—it's Tom Dixon for the Rug Company. So were the modern gray flannel swivel chairs. But the low black marble table between them? $20 at a garage sale.

The signed oil painting from the 1960s: $150 on eBay!

Even my dogs are secondhand! My delicious rescue pups, Harry and Dandy.

The chartreuse in the large vintage oil painting was my inspiration for the pops of bright yellow throughout the first floor. I used variations on the same color palette in each room so they flowed together. I love the contrast of yellow and gray with a pop of turquoise thrown in.

The Emmys in Kathy Griffin's living room are the real deal—NOT a flea market find. (Wouldn't they make great bookends?)

The fuchsia mohair stools were dingy beige chenille when I found them at a thrift shop. Changing the fabric brought them back to life, and chrome tacks made them feel more modern.

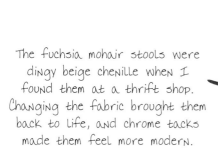

OK, so we know you'll find great, one-of-a-kind pieces by implementing the tips I'll share in this book. But will you find something worthy of your own *Antiques Roadshow* moment? Maybe! During my time hosting *ARS*, I met countless people who have found bona fide treasures on the secondhand circuit. I will show you a few of their finds, and *ARS* expert appraisers Leigh and Leslie Keno will share some of their wisdom with you. And one of my design idols, fellow flea-marketing fiend Jonathan Adler, will share his trade secrets for finding the best "junque."

Did I mention that you are perilously close to becoming addicted to the hunt? Whether you like French country, shabby chic, or mid-century modern, everything you need to create the home of your dreams is out there, waiting to be reinvented, and with this book, I hope to help you find it.

I must warn you: Once you experience the thrill of finding, fixing, and filling your home with one-of-a-kind style, you will never kick this habit. The pull of a yard sale sign will be too much to resist. You will find yourself looking for rooms to redo around your found treasures, and perhaps, if it gets really bad, your habit will result in the need for a storage unit. (That's what happened to me when my husband could no longer fit his car in our garage.)

Look at it this way: You're recycling and reducing landfills, one stylish room at a time, which makes you an environmentalist. Furthermore, you are giving money to those in need every time you shop at a charity thrift store, which means you are something of a philanthropist—and really, what could be more blue blooded than that?

Kathy Griffin's living room. I paid only $135 for the pair of mid-century sofas, but they needed a total overhaul. I reupholstered them in a neutral linen and changed the three foam seat cushions to one down-filled bench cushion. The redo wasn't cheap but still cost much less than she would have paid for just one of these sofas in a shop.

Chapter 1:
Destination: Decoration!
Where Does Your Inner Blue Blood Live?

If you are not sure what your style is, take a peek at how the "other half" lives. I have created five styles, each named for its place of origin, iconic destinations where blue-blood style abounds, and each has its own unique look.

While I really do believe there are no rules in interior design—I much prefer a room with an eclectic mix of styles to one with a uniform look—I do think each of these photos gives off a signature vibe.

Once you determine which feels right for you, you will be able to find loads of ideas throughout this book to arrive at your own personal design destination. Living in these places might cost a pretty penny, but creating the look doesn't have to.

$22

$2.50

The feeling: luxury. The reality: a downright bargain. I painted this $40 thrift-shop chest apple green; the octagonal mirror was also a thrift gift I painted glossy black. The 1960s Lightolier sconces are from 1stdibs.com, and the printed Mylar wallpaper is by Florence Broadhurst.

Style #1
Hollywood to the Hilt

Named for Los Angeles in its golden age, this aesthetic, like movie stars themselves, is built upon glamour and drama. The look calls for Lucite, crystal sconces, faux bamboo mirrors, and slipper chairs. Even though it defined the "Golden" Age of Hollywood, this style is more about cool, silvery tones. Designer William "Billy" Haines is credited with creating the style back in the 1930s, and it lives on today in Hollywood and beyond.

Luminous
Glamorous
SEXY
Luxurious
Decadent

$40

I had a piece of mirror cut to cover the dresser's laminate top, which couldn't be painted. Not only does it hide the laminate, but it adds light and sparkle to the room.

It might be my Connecticut bedroom, but the look is posh, poised, and very Park Avenue. On either side of the king-sized Moroccan-style headboard are vintage neoclassical silver lamps atop painted black French chests. The mix of textures makes it feel grand.

$50

I found this Frenchy-feeling chest at a thrift shop and painted it black.

$95

Style #2
Park Avenue Poise

Numerous books have been written about life on the toniest avenue in all of New York. Studded with stunning prewar buildings containing apartments the size of freestanding homes, there's a reason Park Avenue could just as easily be called "Society Row." Look at the work of Sister Parish, Mark Hampton, and Bunny Williams today, and you see the design thread of eclectic luxury and tailored clutter. The look calls for paisley, animal prints, English antiques, and objets d'art. Park Avenue pedigree is a look that is a little feminine, a little masculine, and totally classic. It's seriously sophisticated but attainable to all with a good eye. You'll see!

Sophisticated
RICH
Classic
Refined
Elegant

Style #3
Greenwich Country Cool

Located on the Connecticut coastline, just thirty miles from New York City, this exclusive bedroom community is home to both old money and new. The style is stately—often equestrian themed in the backcountry section of town, and nautical along the coast. Mahogany, plaid, and leather abound in these chic but cozy rooms. As Tony Duquette so aptly said, "More is more" when it comes to this look. Just like a socialite's man, it's rich and handsome!

Athletic

Masculine

COZY

Aristocratic

Traditional

My Connecticut dining room combines nineteenth-century dog paintings (flea market), a vintage antler chandelier (auction), Chinese ceramic parrots (flea market), and Georgian-style dining chairs (estate sale). I used two Georgian armchairs in yellow leather at the head and foot of the table to make seating for twelve. Painting the ceiling the same green as the walls makes it feel more intimate. It's traditional and clubby but also cozy.

Style #4
Downtown Bohemian

Just a few miles south of the Upper East Side, yet worlds away stylistically, is home to rebellious preppies decamped from their families' Park Avenue pads, on a quest to stretch their hipster wings. The look is an eclectic mix—one part industrial, one part mid-century, with a sprinkling of found objects. Cool without trying. There is perfection in the imperfect. Downtown Bohemian style = free spirit!

Eclectic
HIP
Adventurous
Cool
Industrial

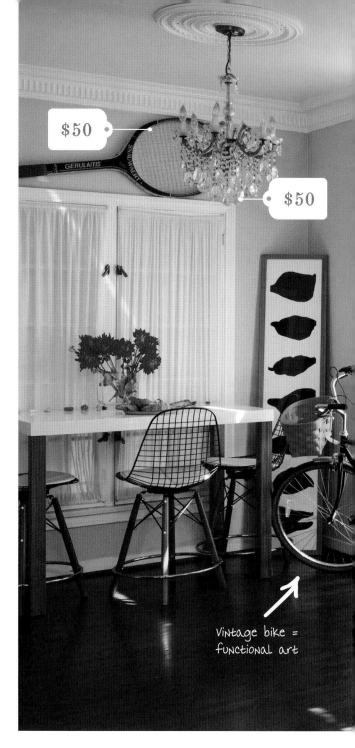

$50

$50

Vintage bike = functional art

$20

Use large
plants for
pops of color

This apartment is quintessentially Downtown Bohemian—even if it is in Hollywood! I found the giant tennis racquet, a vintage store display piece, at the Melrose flea market. The pricey prints came from a friend's atelier in Paris, but the 1970s orange ceramic decanter was a thrift score. With the high/low mix, it all evens out! The bar stools are from Modernica, and the café chairs are by Pottery Barn.

$40

$150

This Danish modern chair I found at the Rose Bowl had nasty upholstery but a snazzy price tag. This same chair goes for $1,750 on 1stDibs.com?

An ottoman doesn't have to be an exact match. Create a mate with matching fabric.

Style #5
Palm Springs Swag

Home-away-from-home to stars in need of a little R & R since the 1930s, Palm Springs is a hot desert paradise whose style is cool and sleek. Envision the Rat Pack sipping martinis in a mid-century man cave and you've got it. While Sinatra, Martin, and Davis Jr. were the names to know on stage, designers Saarinen, Eames, and Baughman lit up the marquees at home. In a swanky Palm Springs room, less is more, and every piece packs a punch.

Spare
Offbeat
SLICK
Modern
Textured

In Kathy Griffin's living room, I used white and black crocodile-embossed vinyl to reupholster the mid-century pieces to make them dog-friendly. The tall-backed Danish modern chair was $350 at the Rose Bowl flea market. The black bench by the window was just $40 at a Beverly Hills estate sale. Martini, anyone?

Good Bones and Good Breeding

When I'm trying to decide whether to buy an item, I first ask myself: Is this something a stylish family would pass down from generation to generation? If you can imagine your fantasy blue-blood clan keeping an item in the family for decades, you can bet it's worth buying. Need more specifics? No matter what its purpose or aesthetic, every piece found in the most fabulous blue-blood homes has two fundamental qualities—just like the most fabulous blue bloods themselves—good bones and good breeding.

Have you ever seen a great beauty and thought, *She could wear a garbage bag and look gorgeous*? That's just how I felt about the fantastic 1950s arm-chairs (on the opposite page)—a major score at just $10 for *all four* at a yard sale! My a-ha moment? Covering them in Pottery Barn laminated shower curtains so they'd be utterly kid-proof at the kitchen table!

A young lady with "good bones" has sharp features, a nice profile, and an overall eye-catching appeal. Things are really no different when it comes to furniture. Solid construction, iconic shapes, great details—these are the things that make a piece worthy of your soon to be not-so-humble abode.

The saying "don't judge a book by its cover" is spot-on here. Sometimes one must look past a scuffed finish or dirty upholstery in order to see the magic beneath. Cosmetic flaws are easily fixed; structural problems are not. Good bones are one thing, but good breeding takes a piece to a whole new level. In blue-blood speak, it means a person comes from a good family. When it comes to furniture, it means the piece was born from the workshop of an iconic designer or manufacturer. If you can find a tag or signature to prove a piece's origin, your find might have more than high style. It might be high quality and worth passing down.

The hand-painted family crest is a dead giveaway that this isn't just any butter dish. Closer inspection revealed it's nineteenth-century English porcelain, probably made for some fabulous blue blood. I wonder if they would be horrified to know their coat of arms now lives in my fridge?

Upholstery tacks, in chrome or brass, shiny or matte, are a stylish way to embellish an upholstery job— and hide unsightly seams.

Pottery Barn shower curtains— heavy-duty plastic—only $11.99 each. All you need is one per chair!

After re-covering my kitchen chairs for the umpteenth time (little kids make big messes), I decided to try laminated shower curtains to cover them. The result is undeniably hip and indestructible!

Clues to Quality

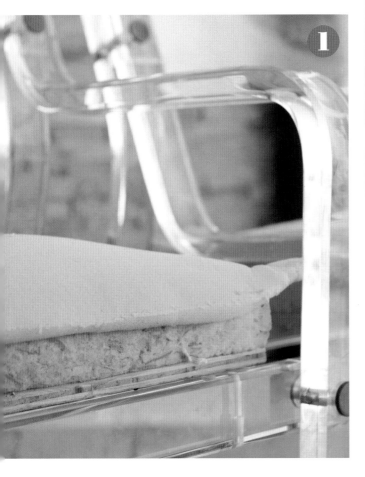

Get past a piece's tragic current state and ask yourself:

• Is it hefty or flimsy?

• Does it have handcrafted details?

• Does it have iconic, period style?

Here are some examples of what to look for.

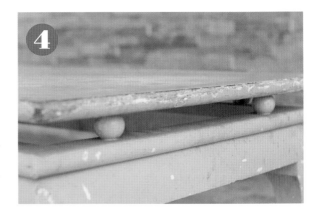

1. This Lucite chair was a major score, though it doesn't look like much here, with its crumbly foam seat exposed. I found a pair of these at a thrift shop for $150 and could see by the thick Lucite and brass rivets they had great bones. Turns out they are Charles Hollis Jones chairs and retail for $3,500 at high-end antique shops! (See page 101 for the after).

2. Look for classic motifs such as the Greek key detail on this vintage Baker chest. A yard sale steal for $300 (also see page 156 for the "after").

3. Good bones, literally! This late eighteenth-century estate sale find has an ivory escutcheon.

4. The Asian details and solid, heavy wood of this vintage coffee table are worth a lot more than the $5 I paid for it at an estate sale. Yes, I know it looks like a $5 table, but check out page 140.

$80

$5

Katharine Hepburn could make khakis look couture. How? Because if you have good bones, you can wear anything. The dingy damask couldn't hide the beauty of this Georgian high-back wing chair—$80 at a tag sale—and like Kate Hepburn's, its good bones allow this chair to "wear" anything, even hot pink faux croc! (An upholstery choice made by *my* Kate the Great, my six-year-old daughter.)

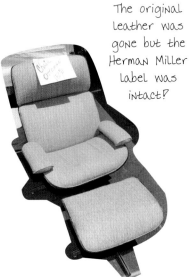

The original leather was gone but the Herman Miller label was intact!

If this occasional table, priced at $100 at the Rose Bowl flea market, had a label identifying it as made by Eero Saarinen, it would have been twice the price.

$200

$150

Too good to be true? A Ray and Charles Eames lounge chair and ottoman for just $150 at the Rose Bowl. Re-covered in white leather, the pair is easily worth ten times what I paid! The Louis Vuitton poster was also a flea find.

Lesson I: Due Diligence

Be an investigator: Lift cushions, look at the underside of tables, open drawers. Just as a father looks over prospective suitors for his beautiful daughter, you need to give any pieces you are considering living with a major once-over. Due diligence means taking the time to look under the hood, so to speak, for manufacturer's markings. That said, you must hone your eye. Tags do come off, so it's important to become familiar with the hallmarks of a quality manufacturer's work. You can do this by browsing websites like 1stdibs.com or reading descriptions of pieces you like in antique shops or auction catalogs. That's the advice I got from the appraisers on *Antiques Roadshow*, and it has been invaluable.

MAKER'S MARK

It's not just the whiskey of choice among society types. It's also the monogram, logo, or label that identifies a furnishing's maker.

You can't beat Baker. The set of four vintage barrel-back chairs to the right was manufactured by Baker Furniture, as you can see from the elegant woven label I found under the seat cushion. They cost me $150 for all four at an estate sale. Baker is a name you want to look for. They have been making high-quality contemporary furniture and elegant antique reproductions since 1890.

Early cabinetmakers often signed their pieces on the underside of a drawer. Today the mark can often be found inside a drawer, usually one on top, on the side. The sideboard below, which you will see in its new coat of paint later in this book, was made by Drexel, probably in the 1960s. Drexel is another American manufacturer of classic styles, founded in North Carolina in 1903.

Check out page 139 to see how my $79 buffet looks now and page 161 to see the burnt-orange Baker chairs come to life.

Sometimes a girl gets lucky, finding a piece she adores, then discovering that it's marked with the name or logo of a well-known artist or architect. It's like falling in love with a handsome man you think is penniless, and then finding out he's heir to a fortune!

Lesson 2: Diamond in the Rough…or Just Rough?

As every proper lady knows, so much of one's success in life depends on one's ability to say (politely) no. Not every piece—no matter how gorgeous—wants to be rescued. Remember *Peyton Place*? Sometimes the prettiest girls led the most sordid lives, and no matter how many well-meaning meddlers tried to hold them together, they fell apart. Make sure there are no hidden problems with your find. I'm not interested in procuring anything with any of these skeletons in its closet, and you shouldn't be, either.

- Chairs with very loose arms
- Case furniture with cracked or broken legs (like a stallion, she'll never be the same again)
- Wood pieces whose veneer is pulling away
- Lucite pieces with lots of scratches—you will always see them
- Chipped or cracked pottery, unless you really like it. The integrity is compromised, and repairs are costly and cannot be guaranteed.

It's not a bargain if it has bedbugs. Leave street couches right where you find them, and be sure to inspect upholstered secondhand pieces carefully.

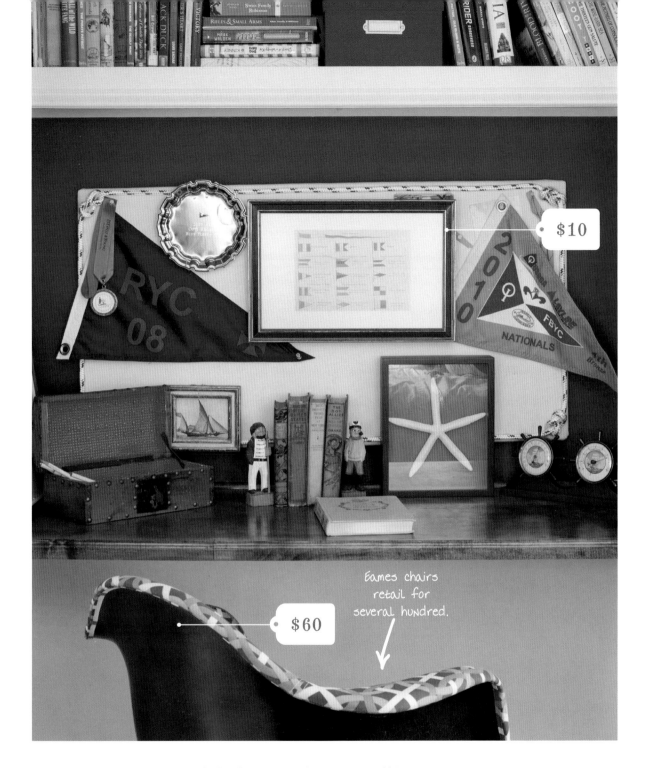

$10

$60

Eames chairs
retail for
several hundred.

Eames-ing High: Why not use a seriously chic chair in a young boy's room? I couldn't save the original hopsack upholstery on this authentic Eames shell chair, but for $60, it was worth the $100 I spent to re-cover it in a groovy blue Sunbrella fabric that will be resistant to snacks and markers. In keeping with the room's nautical theme, an old wooden "treasure chest" becomes a pencil box, and carved salty-dog figures act as bookends. All of the accessories were found at thrift shops and flea markets, and none were more than $15!

Even the smallest apartment deserves a proper bar.

The silver-rimmed rocks glasses (same as the ones used on *Mad Men*) were just $2 each at a thrift shop.

Mary Meade's
Magic
Recipes
for the
Electric
Blender
by Ruth Ellen Church

OPPOSITE: The clock on the bar lets my friend Rebecca know when it's happy hour! Look for vintage rolling carts, like this 1960s Lucite version I found for $100. The clock had an ugly cord when I bought it for $10, so I took it to an appliance store and had it changed to battery-powered. Thrift shops are also a great place to buy vintage barware for next to nothing. I bought the 1960s bartending guide because I loved the color, but the truth is, it has some great recipes in it!

Name Dropper

Look for vintage pieces made by the following manufacturers and designers—their reputations for quality go without saying.

BAKER	KITTINGER
DREXEL	VERNER PANTON
HENREDON	PARZINGER
JAMES MONT	KARL SPRINGER
WILLIAM HAINES	

Like a core group of best friends, these tried-and-true pieces will always be welcome in your home. Some girls covet shoes. Me? I love chairs. Big, small, high, low, curvy, straight, cushy, or hard. Here are a few trustworthy favorites to keep your eye out for. Their shapes are classic, so they work in almost any interior. With a little paint or new fabric, what seems stuffy can suddenly be sassy.

The straight, tapered leg on the wing chair makes it sleek and masculine enough for an office or living room, or to anchor the heads of a long dining table.

This diminutive club chair
is the opposite of today's
super-sized versions. Its size
makes it cozy, comfortable,
and classic.

Side chairs, like this faux bamboo and
cane version, can be used as hall chairs,
alongside a sideboard, or flanking a fireplace. Great for standby seating. These
look good painted almost any color.

The deco-style upholstered armchair
would work in Palm Springs if it were done
in white leather, or on Park Avenue if it
were done in kelly green mohair. These
armchairs are versatile team players you
can use anywhere.

THE
Inner Circle
Cocktail Tables

Put two together as a coffee table, or saddle one up next to a club chair to hold a tall glass of champagne. The side table is an indispensable ingredient to blue-blood decor.

Small trunks make great drinks tables and double as storage.

Nesting tables provide three spots for the space of one; clear Lucite keeps the focus on the more important pieces in the room.

Make sure your drinks table is never taller than the armchair or sofa it's next to.

3

Chinese garden stools make great side tables—indoors or out. No one will ever forget this little elephant!

4

The inner circle, indeed! A fresh coat of red paint woke up this faux-bamboo sleeper.

5

The cube was painted a horrible shade of green when I bought it for $5 at a yard sale, but the shape was so cool, and the height was just right.

Chapter 2: Working the Scene

Just as socialistas (otherwise known as the "in-crowd") know which parties to attend, bargainistas know how to work the sale circuit each weekend, in order to get maximum blue-blood bang for their blue-collar buck.

If you think it's tough keeping up with the Joneses, wait until you get a load of a dedicated treasure hunter's weekend schedule. On any given Saturday, Sunday—or most any other day of the week, really—those in the know will hit yard sales, garage sales, and estate sales at private homes. While these sorts of sales have fixed and finite dates, flea markets recur regularly. Chances are, a top hunter will fill his "empty" days—read: the rest of the week—with trips to his favorite thrift and charity stores, which most likely have regular working hours.

1. Just like my mom did with me, here I am with my own kids, circling the next day's yard sale ads that look appealing and mapping out our plan of attack. Another generation of hunters is born!

2. One of the many garage sale signs that hang all over Los Angeles every weekend.

3. The UCLA thrift shop benefits the university's medical auxiliary.

4. Just a sampling of the thousands of items being sold at Clarke Auction Gallery in Larchmont, New York.

5. Bonham's Sunset Estate auctions in Los Angeles offer something for everyone.

6. A sign at the Elephant's Trunk Flea Market in New Milford, Connecticut.

7. A ceramic "bamboo" lamp catches my eye at a local thrift store.

The Deal Circuit

- Everybody wins at charity thrift shops. They have great prices, benefit worthy causes, and tend to hold pretty regular business hours. I have found some of my favorite pieces at thrift shops, and love knowing that each time I buy a piece, my money is going toward a great cause. Donations often come from well-to-do families with a connection to that shop's benefactor.

- Sales at private homes (yard, sidewalk, garage, and estate sales) usually have the best prices, but shopping them can also require a lot of work sifting through used toys, broken appliances, and out-of-date clothing. The whole thing can be a little scary, and yet somehow intoxicating! Flea market dealers shop yard and estate sales, often buying entire contents of homes, which they then turn around and sell at a markup.

- Flea market pricing is usually slightly higher than yard and estate sales, but because there's less junk to sift through, you are paying for a more curated shopping experience.

- Parallel to flea markets are auctions. While many people think of auctions as too hoity-toity for anyone but the superrich, this couldn't be further from the truth. All manner of antiques, art, rugs, and tchotchkes can be had for a steal at an auction—which is often a fascinating piece of social theater in its own right.

All in a day's work. Here I am with just one day's haul from the flea market in Long Beach, California. A vintage school map of the United States, an old abacus, a wooden ladder, a wall clock, a railroad sign, a mahogany chair, a console table, an oil painting of a horse, and brass fish lamps. All of it cost me under $350!

What to Bring

First and foremost . . . cash! Nothing kills a negotiation like the phrase, "Will you take a check?"

Something to schlep your haul home in. Remember, this isn't Nordstrom, so don't look for shopping bags or tissue wrap. You're lucky if you get a flimsy grocery bag from most dealers or thrift stores. This is part of the "charm" of the experience. I always bring a giant canvas bag.

Old newspaper—or bubble wrap, if you are really ambitious—to protect fragile items, as well as an empty box or two in which to nestle them safely for the drive home.

Collapsible wire cart. You can find them at any chain store, and sometimes they even sell them at the flea market! They should cost no more than $10 or $15 but are priceless for what they save you in back pain.

Tape measure. You won't believe how obsessed you will become with measuring things.

A notebook containing:
- A list of what you're hunting for (it's shockingly easy to forget)
- Any important measurements or dimensions, e.g., the depth of the nook you're looking to fill with a bookcase or the size of a piece of art you'd like to frame
- Tearsheets: The gorgeous interiors in *Elle Décor* and other shelter mags are your design blueprint, showing you the pieces to look for to create your magazine-worthy room. It's all there for you: makers, eras, styles. Use this information to create your own shopping wish list.

Baby wipes or antibacterial hand gel, because sometimes things can get a little . . . sticky.

Smartphone, if possible, so that you can perform feverish searches for information or pricing on items, send photos to friends and/or consultants for emergency opinions, or call your emergency contact and beg them to bring more cash!

LEFT: These vintage metal lamps, shaped like yachting buoys, were perfect for the nautical-themed boys' room my friend was doing for her sons. We bought the lamps at a flea market for $25 each.

BELOW: Tickled Pink! It's survived intact since the 1960s. It would have been a shame for this incredible Murano Art Glass bowl to become a casualty of an overzealous flea market outing. The antique cement dog stands guard at my front door.

What to Look For

You will get tons of ideas in the following chapters, but if I had to give you a shopping list of classic pieces that will work in a room of any style, here's what would be on it:

- unique lamps—a great way to add color and interest to a room
- mirrors—you can never have enough to add light and glamour
- pairs of Foo dogs (or any dogs, for that matter) to flank an entrance or fireplace
- original art—doesn't matter if it has any value. If you love it, buy it and retire your mass-produced prints!

The idea is to make your home feel as if it has been put together over time in a life well lived. And remember: Symmetry is stylish. If you see two of something, take both! Pairs of anything are almost always better than one.

Animal Magnetism

I am always on the hunt for animals—specifically, dogs, stags, horses, elephants, and the occasional owl. And it's not just me! They're ubiquitous in blue-blood decor. (Show me a blue-blood who doesn't love a horse print, and I'll show you a liar.)

The '40s neoclassical style club chair, vintage wicker table, bronze dolphin lamp and '60s oil painting create the feeling of a space assembled over generations. In reality, every piece was found at either an estate sale or flea market.

TALE OF A
Chair

Great Aunt Bootsie was given a delicate nineteenth-century French bergère chair as a wedding gift. It had been in her husband's family for generations. It served her traditional Park Avenue style well until she went all Space Age in 1960. Though she no longer needed it, she still felt attached. She passed the little bergère down to her daughter, Bitsey, who thought it would look simply charming in her dorm room at Columbia.

She tried to give it an update, replacing the toile fabric with zany zebra stripes and a coat of pink paint. Then, hating it just as her poor mother said she would, she sold it at her sorority's charity yard sale.

Bitsey's Bohemian cousin Cricket stopped by the sale and snapped it up for a song! It was perfect for her new loft in SoHo (her family kept Cricket's new location hush-hush—not exactly where nice girls from the Upper East Side went to live in the sixties!). Cricket wanted a sleeker look, though, so she lacquered the chair in high-gloss black.

The chair lived in harmony with the loft's other eclectic furnishings—that is, until Cricket met Walter the financier, who was less into the Warhol Factory than the Nixon White House. He convinced her to donate the chair to the hospital thrift shop down the street from their new Westchester home (tax deduction!).

Lulie, a young suburban housewife and budding interior designer, noticed the sad little chair in the thrift shop window and saw beyond the flawed finish. Recognizing the great bones beneath its many coats of paint, she stripped it to reveal its beautiful walnut frame. She covered it in clean white linen, giving it a place of honor in her well-edited home.

Years later, when our dear Lulie found success as a society decorator, Hollywood beckoned and she brought the chair to a high-end antique shop to sell on consignment. A lesser-known decorator

convinced her client to pay a pretty penny for the well-restored piece and installed it in her gracious Greenwich home, where it encountered nary a bottom for years in the very formal living room.

As we all know, though, tastes change, as do husbands. So when Mrs. X, as we'll call her, divorced and remarried new money, she hired a maverick decorator to replace all her wood and velvet with chrome and suede.

She put the chair up for auction at a very prestigious house, making sure the description included the chair's provenance—that it came directly from

the personal collection of the now world-renowned interior designer to the stars, Lulie Sinclaire.

The bidders, though, were not as impressed as she had hoped, for they had fallen for chrome and suede too. Because the chair offered neither, John, a dashing young fellow with an eye for Versailles, grabbed it on the cheap and sat proudly upon it in his West Village bachelor pad—until he was swept off his feet by his own dashing financier.

When the happy couple abandoned John's

modest nest for a Hong Kong skyscraper, John's landlord inherited his modest possessions. This had happened before—fickle New Yorkers—and Mr. Price knew what to do.

With a storage room filled with former tenants' castoffs, he set up shop at the Hell's Kitchen flea market on a chilly Sunday morning. He priced the silly little chair at just $10—what did he know?—delighting Amy, the design blogger who recognized it from a back issue of *House & Garden* in an article about her favorite decorator, the aforementioned Ms. Sinclaire.

Still paying off her student loans, Amy decided to post the article—and the chair—on eBay, where she knew she could make some design junkie's day, as well as a hefty profit. She got $150 for her $10 investment, which sounded divine to dear Amy, but as both you and I know, is really next-to-nothing for a chair with good bones and an incredible pedigree.

So many pieces I find have stories like this. Or, at least, I imagine they do. Remember: At the end of the day, even the finest antique is expensive, really good quality used furniture.

The Decorationary

As-Is

Broken, scuffed, chipped . . . but too cool to toss. Full disclosure usually means a major discount, but you're buying it with the knowledge that it'll never be perfect—and that you will not be permitted to return it.

Barcelona Chair

An iconic black leather seat designed by architect Ludwig Mies van der Rohe in 1929. Found in the toniest apartment-building lobbies since its conception.

Biedermeier

German furniture style from the first half of the 1800s. Aimed to bring the materials and Romanticism of the outside world into the home. Often with painted details in gold or black.

Cantilevered

A piece of furniture designed to look as though it is somehow floating—a design ambition common to the mid-century period. Supported just from one side.

Consignment

An agreement whereby a store sells merchandise that belongs to someone else (the "consignor") and they split the proceeds. Some antique and resale stores operate this way, so in addition to buying stuff from them, you can sell stuff through them too.

Deadstock

New merchandise—e.g., rolls of fabric—that has been sitting in a warehouse for years and years, sometimes decades. A decorator's fantasy time capsule.

Escutcheon

An ornamental plate protecting a keyhole. And an awesomely obscure word you can pull out at cocktail parties.

Firm

Nonnegotiable. As in, do not ask for a better price.

Foxing

The cloudy spots that occur on very old mirrors as a result of oxidation.

Lattice

A crisscross pattern popular in designer fabrics from the 1960s and 1970s.

Lucite

The brand name of a transparent plastic resin. Can also be referred to by its other brand names Plexiglas or Perspex, or generically speaking, "acrylic." Quality varies from type to type—some kinds scratch more easily than others, for example.

Net Price

A dealer is charging you what they paid—sans markup—most likely because they've had an item too long.

No Reserve

The buying market decides what an item is worth—it will be sold for the highest amount offered, no matter how low this amount is.

Objets d'Art

The WASP term for tchotchkes.

Patina

The charming evidence of wear and tear that makes vintage pieces just look, well, better than new ones. Fading, crackling, discoloration—an inanimate object's version of smile lines. It's what signals a history and gives a piece character.

Picker

Someone who earns their living "picking" through yard sales, flea markets, thrift shops, abandoned mansions . . . looking for unique and hopefully valuable pieces to resell.

Remnant

Leftover piece of material that a fabric or carpet store sells for next to nothing. Too small for an upholsterer or pro decorator to use, a remnant is often the perfect size for a small project—and you can find incredibly high-end brands for as little as $5!

Saddle Seat

A chair with a seat contoured to fit the curves of the human bum.

Slat Back

A wooden chair with a back formed of horizontal pieces of wood attached to two side posts.

Slip Seat

A removable upholstered seat common to dining chairs. Easy to re-cover.

Smalls

Term used at auction houses and multidealer centers to describe items usually kept in a case. Figurines, vintage boxes, ceramics—you know . . . small stuff.

Splat Back

A wooden chair with a central wood panel that extends from the seat to the top of the back, supporting the spine.

To-the-Trade

A discount given to professional decorators who have a resale tax number, usually ranging between 10 and 30 percent.

Veneer

A wood treatment where the heavy frame of a piece of furniture is covered by two sheets of thin, shiny, decorative wood.

Vintage

Anything older than new. A gentle way to say "used"!

Chapter 3:
Estate Planning

First of all, let's just get this out there.

YARD SALE = **TAG SALE** = **GARAGE SALE** = **ESTATE SALE**

They are all generally the same thing—people selling unwanted things from private homes.

An estate sale is basically a garage sale held in a fancy house. But there is something about that word—"estate"— that gets me every time. Maybe it's the connotation of a grand manor filled with a lifetime's worth of collections— covered in dust, waiting for me to save them.

Estate Dates

I always check the classifieds of the local paper on Thursdays. There is usually a section for sales, and most run Fridays to Sundays. You can also troll craigslist.com and estatesales.net to see what's coming up for the weekend.

Strategize your Saturdays and Sundays. Make a route map the night before the morning of the sale—even drive it for practice if you can. Minutes mean everything if you're trying to snag that Eames chair—you want to grab it before everybody else tells the seller what it's really worth. While many hard-core thrifters insist that everything good is gone before 10 A.M., I still go to sales later in the day, when the sellers are motivated to drop prices.

Of course, even if you're not a planner, you can slam on the brakes—like my mom—every time you see a sign on Saturday mornings.

Contrary to popular belief, an estate sale doesn't always mean there is one less WASP in the world. In fact, a good portion of them are people downsizing, relocating, or redecorating—so don't be totally creeped out.

Plus, if it *is* an estate selling the contents of their deceased loved one's home, the family is usually at peace with it. They have gone through and taken what they want, and they are usually happy to see pieces that meant a lot to the person who passed away live on in another nice home. Hopefully . . . yours!

INSIDER TIP

The nicer the neighborhood, the nicer the junk!

Mahogany side table $20!

OPPOSITE: This gracious home in Brentwood, California, was chock-full of Continental furnishings and goodies, many of which you will see on the next few pages.

THIS PAGE: This estate sale in Los Angeles was held at the home of a lifelong collector. You name it, it was for sale. And there were bargains galore! Don't be afraid to dig, and try to imagine pieces in a new setting, free from the clutter.

FASHIONS *fade*— **STYLE** *is* **ETERNAL**

YVES SAINT LAURENT

Be a Design Detective

Read between the lines. If the newspaper ad boasts "loads of kids' toys," "baby clothes," or "tons of tools," you probably won't find that James Mont sideboard you so covet. If the ad mentions "vintage collectibles," "mid-century," and "antique furniture," it is worth exploring—and if you see an ad that reads anything like "lifelong collector clearing out," get in your car and *go*!

The exterior of a house will tell you almost everything you need to know about what will be for sale. Let's say you're going for a streamlined, 1960s aesthetic. If you see a mid-century house, it will likely have some mid-century stuff. Plan to hit that house first thing in the day since it suits your aesthetic and you want access to the best scores.

A Colonial-style house will usually have more traditional stuff for sale, so if you collect American antiques, stop at this house first. My point? People tend to decorate based on the architectural vibe of their house; for example, a Mediterranean house will likely have a more European flair than a 1960s glass-and-steel one.

Advanced shoppers can look for further clues than the house's exterior: Is there an old sedan in the driveway, or a brand-new minivan? One means treasures, the other means terrible twos. Put your Nancy Drew hat on.

Big, new houses rarely have treasures to spare. If the people haven't lived in their home for a long time, they won't have much to get rid of. So stick to older neighborhoods, not newer subdivisions. Learn to do a slow and thorough drive-by before you park and commit. Generally, when I see a pile of toys lining the front lawn, I usually just drive on. A younger family will be selling their Pack 'n Plays, not their Picassos.

This vignette was assembled from three different sales, all at groovy houses.

$160

$20
for two

$70   Plus $150
       to re-cover

$39

$200

The wooden masks were one of those "not sure where I'll use them, but they are so cool!" moments!

MAYBE IT'S NOT HOME SWEET HOME ADJUST

Any lampshade can be converted into a hanging light. Just ask your electrician.

It's time to mix it up! From Africa to Paris to New England, this kitchen is a great example of how ethnic pieces, fine antiques, and one-of-a-kind finds can work together to form a unified look. The nineteenth-century farm table is a family heirloom. I found the 1920s clock at an estate sale, and the copper pot centerpiece was a yard sale bargain.

Estate $ale Etiquette

Everybody knows the saying "You catch more flies with honey than vinegar." Well, at estate sales, the sweeter you are to the staff, the sweeter the deals you'll score. Alla Smushkevich, who runs Paragon Estate Sales in Los Angeles, has seen the good, the bad, and the downright rude.

Here are her tips on estate sale etiquette:

- Be polite. No cracking jokes about the decor. Family members are often present at the sale.

- Prices are usually nonnegotiable at the beginning of the sale—you can always ask for a better deal, but be respectful if the answer is no.

- If prices are too firm for your taste, ask about end-of-sale discounts—which can slash up to 50 percent off. Remember, the family is trying to empty the house. If you are not afraid of possibly losing a piece you like, it might be worth waiting to see if it comes down in price.

- Remember: The person running the sale is working for the family—who dictates the pricing—so don't get mad at the staff!

- Do not ask for a better price on anything under $5.

- Twenty people are allowed inside at a time in homes that contain valuable pieces—cutting, pushing, or whining will result in you being asked to leave.

- If you want to purchase a piece that's too large to carry around, remove its tag and bring it to the checkout person. Let them know you are taking it so no one else does!

- This is not *Supermarket Sweep*. Don't grab items or tickets unless you are serious about buying them—it's not fair to other shoppers, the family, or those running the sale.

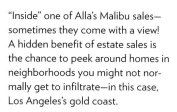

"Inside" one of Alla's Malibu sales—sometimes they come with a view! A hidden benefit of estate sales is the chance to peek around homes in neighborhoods you might not normally get to infiltrate—in this case, Los Angeles's gold coast.

$10
Each

$20

This '60s tuxedo sofa had great bones

These nineteenth-century British prints came from a dusty box in a lovely old lady's backyard. I hung them over the sofa in a grid pattern to form one show-stopping art piece. The lamp is part of a pair I bought at Goodwill for $19.99, and the sofa was $150 at an L.A. charity thrift shop. I re-covered it in soft, cocoa-colored velvet.

This table and chairs looked frumpy in their former home because of the other furnishings in the room. Try to imagine your finds in a younger, fresher space. It changes everything.

Don't judge a chair by its cover. Kathy Griffin had an empty corner in her living room that just needed something and this estate sale find—a 1950s mahogany games table and chairs—did the trick. You'd never guess the chairs were formerly frumpy. Thank God Kathy didn't see them before I recovered them in silver leather. A little polish on the brass and a coat of black paint on the legs, and they were ready to roll.

Things that sparkle and shine draw light into any space. Mirrors, Lucite, chrome, crystal . . . the more, the better!

$50

My estate sale score! One of four Baker chairs re-covered in chartreuse velvet.

A 1960s Vladimir Kagan coffee table—$600 on eBay, a fraction of its retail value!

The Scene Setter

Sometimes a single piece can inspire the decor of a whole room. In my family room, the three panels of vintage Gracie hand-painted wallpaper dictated the opulent color scheme and vibe. I found the panels at a Connecticut estate sale, leftover from someone's high-end home makeover. There weren't enough to cover a full wall—so I framed them! Check out GracieStudio.com to see more of their incredible wall coverings.

Any inside scoop you can pick up about the people having the sale is useful. I was recently tipped off about a moving sale at the home of a very stylish couple, one of whom is a major antique collector, and the other, an artist and set designer.

Is your heartbeat quickening? For years, the couple had been addicted to hunting for more and more treasures, and one day, they just decided they were done. They wanted to go in a different direction with their new house, so everything was for sale—out with the old! Because there was sooooo much stuff to get rid of, the couple knew they needed to keep prices down in order to move the goods. In situations such as this one, be willing to look everywhere. Go through closets and boxes—don't be afraid to dig.

OK, so smoking is passé, but ashtrays make great candy dishes and also look great as part of a tabletop tableau. This turquoise ashtray, probably swiped from a Paris restaurant, says *bon vivant*!

$1

Survey the 'scape

Look for cool, quirky pieces to create great tablescapes. A mix of big and small, silly and serious—you want these vignettes to reflect the people, places, and things you love.

I scored this unusual tole lamp direct from the bedroom it had been illuminating for fifty-plus years. Taken out of the time warp and into the open, it became something special.

A French roulette wheel, circa 1940, is a one-of-a-kind find. Bought at a Bel Air estate sale, it's got great colors for a preppy, clubby interior and it comes in handy at parties! It even came in its original box, with scorecards written in French. *Oui oui*!

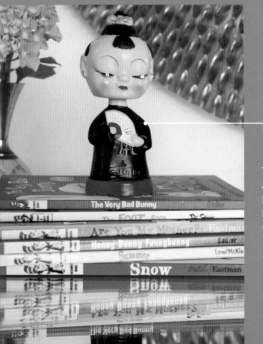

$2

This 1950s bobblehead is always agreeable. Random, I know—but I couldn't resist. Look in boxes at flea markets— that's where I found her for $2!

More Is More

Scattering collections around a space will make the pieces look like random clutter. Instead, group collections or like objects to create a focal point. Remember: There is power in numbers.

Chapter 4: That Flea-ting Moment

Do I buy it? Or should I keep looking? At flea markets, this question represents the moment of truth. It's what separates the women from the hoarders. If you want the good stuff, you need to go for it. OK, so you might end up with a few things that don't exactly fit—but that's what storage units are for! I joke. If it's really special, you'll find a spot for it. . . . As my girlfriends and I always say, "You snooze, you lose."

What we mean is, if you hesitate, you need to understand there is a good chance the piece won't be there when you get back.

I know the name "flea market" isn't very appealing—and yes, these open-air bazaars where secondhand items are sold were nicknamed for the very reason you think. But before you recoil in horror, rest assured: After just one visit, the only itch you'll feel is the one to come back!

Market Research

You can thank the Internet for making it wildly easy to find flea markets in your area. Just type "flea market" and your ZIP code into any search engine and you'll find a list. (Check out my Little Black Filofax on page 173 for more specifics.) Flea markets take a little more planning in terms of weather and time than do sales at private homes, but they are well worth the effort. Yes, prices might be slightly higher, but your chances of finding great things are also better.

As I said earlier, the sellers at flea markets do the curating for you. Many of them go to the very estate and yard sales I told you about in the last chapter, weeding out the Barbies and Big Wheels on a mission for the good stuff. So, rather than driving from yard sale to estate sale, at flea markets you get one-stop shopping. We're talking acres of aristocratic castoffs waiting to be reinvented. Sure, you will pay slightly more for the convenience—but time is money, right?

Set your alarm. The early bird gets the worm, and at flea markets, you pay for the privilege. Most will charge you a little bit extra to get in early. At one of my favorites, the Elephant's Trunk in New Milford, Connecticut, entrance costs $1 at 7 A.M., but if you want to go as early as 5 A.M., it will cost you $20! Hunting at dawn is not for everyone.

INSIDER TIP

Check the weather report. Most flea markets are outside! Keep an umbrella and some sunblock in your car to brave the elements.

LEFT: Inspecting a Lucite vanity bench before I pull the trigger. Marcos Lima is one of my favorite dealers at the Rose Bowl. I always head to his booth first for fabulous mid-century finds.

RIGHT: Would Kelly Wearstler wear this? Doubtful, but fashion had to take a backseat on this rainy flea market visit. I broke my own rule and forgot to check the weather the night before, so a Hefty bag had to double as rain gear.

OPPOSITE: My home away from home every second Sunday of the month. I go so much, they gave me a special VIP card for frequent flea-ers. I am not joking.

Time Is Money

- If you're going to be one of the first people at the flea market, remember that you might even beat the sun! Bring a jacket, a thermos of hot coffee, and a flashlight. Seriously.

- Become a regular. Acquaint yourself with where your favorite dealers set up. For example, at the Elephant's Trunk, I head straight for the last row—the territory of my favorite dealers—and work my way to the front. The fact that I prioritize them motivates the chosen ones to give me their best deals and pieces.

- Wait until the very last minute to negotiate a deal on something, since the last thing a dealer wants is to have to pack things back up.

- Ask for free delivery if a dealer is unwilling to come down on price. Many dealers are happy to make the drive if it means getting a big object—or a big-ticket item—off their hands.

In Los Angeles, the Pasadena Rose Bowl is my favorite flea market. It boasts a huge selection, fair prices, and a slew of famous faces on any given Sunday. People are willing to brave strong sun and crowds because you can literally decorate your entire house with the vintage finds you come across here. (For this reason, it's every Hollywood set decorator's favorite resource.)

PIES

LEMON

CHOCOLATE

CREAM

CUSTARD

COCOANUT

PUMPKIN

APPLE

PINEAPPLE

BERRY

...CH

...DING

...LA MODE

...RRY

...HORTCAKE

FRUIT JELLO

It's a briefcase . . . or is it?

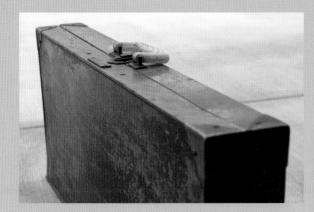

One of my favorite and most unusual discoveries: a fold-up picnic table from the 1940s. It is the kind of find that works outside or in an industrial kitchen or living room. This one-of-a-kind find was just $40 at a flea market.

Unusual finds that prove it's crucial to think outside the box.

LEFT: Small unique objects like this 1875 Swiss cowbell add interest to bookshelves and coffee tables. Also look for old, leather-bound books. They are usually very inexpensive and create a rich, layered look.

BELOW: A hand-painted Japanese puppet head, found at an L.A. flea market.

They may not tell you this, but flea market dealers expect you to negotiate. So do it!

You Won't Find These at Ikea!

I have seen incredible finds go directly from a flea market to a high-end antique shop. And the only thing that changes? The price tag. But finding those great pieces takes work, and navigating the seemingly endless aisles can be overwhelming and intimidating. My strategy is to walk the entire market once, of course shopping along the way, but really, to get a lay of the land. Then I do a second pass and really start to examine the different booths and tables. Sometimes I don't notice key pieces until my third lap!

What does one do with circa 1900 sock stretchers? Kick up those heels and create a groovy art piece for a girl's room! That's what!

$10

These vintage metal letters I bought at the Rose Bowl for $20 apiece actually came off an old building in Pasadena. It's a recycled monogram! The "H" stands for "Happy Home."

Set of mid-century nesting tables, a 1950s diner sign . . . just a snapshot of the variety of vintage accessories you can find at flea markets!

The monogram is part of blue-blood life—use vintage letters from old signs to personalize your space.

Mirror, Mirror on the Wall: Why Can't I See Myself at All?

In even the swankiest of circles, everyone knows the best characters are usually the most flawed. The same is true for mirrors. It was my mom who taught me that the spottiness that often befalls old mirrors—called "foxing"—is not a defect, but an asset.

If the mercury on the back of old glass is oxidizing, probably due to heat or moisture, that doesn't mean you need to swap out the glass. If you want a clear reflection, go buy a newer mirror. But don't replace the glass, even if it's nearly impossible to see yourself. These foxy old gals have real value, and replacing any part will hurt that immensely.

A woman's intuition is rarely wrong. If you love something, buy it.

The smoky, silvery glow of the hundred-year-old mirror below makes it even more desirable to decorators and dealers. New glass would take away all the charm.

If you love something, buy it. If you second guess and walk away to "think about it," like I did from this great C. Jeré-style sunburst mirror, be prepared not to see it when you get back. (Of course this one was gone! It was only $80!) I liked this mirror so much I took a picture of it. It's still a painful reminder. OK, so I'm being a little bit dramatic, but it really was a great piece.

Let's Take the HAG Out of Haggling

(THE DOS AND DON'TS OF NEGOTIATING)

Do ask for a better price. People who run yard, tag, and estate sales, and deal at flea markets expect you to negotiate—so do it!

Do remember that cash is king and makes every deal more attractive.

Do always try to act calm. I never show my excitement over something, even if I'm jumping for joy deep down inside. I look at it and casually ask the price. When I am genuinely interested in buying an item, my standard lines include respectfully asking, "Is that your best price?" and "Can you do any better?" If the dealer says no, you need to make a choice. How badly do you want the item? Do you *need* it, or are you buying on impulse? And how hard is it to find whatever it is you are considering? Is this a one-of-a-kind opportunity, or is there a good likelihood you will see something like it again? If yes, then perhaps you should walk away.

Don't be a hag. The idea is to pay less, not lose the item altogether just because the seller can't stand dealing with you (and believe me, this happens).

Don't fawn over an item. Never admit how much you love something! Saying, "Oh my God I've been looking for one of these for years" kind of weakens your negotiating power.

Don't exclaim, "Wow! That is so cheap" when the dealer tells you the price of something you want. Again, it's a bit harder to ask for a better price when you already told the person what a great deal you think it is.

Don't regret it. I've usually been filled with regret by not buying something I truly loved just because the dealer wouldn't haggle. It's easy to get caught up in the adrenaline of the moment, but take a deep breath and consider how much you would expect to pay for it at a store. Usually, even without an additional discount, you're probably getting a bargain.

A-List Home

This view of Kathy Griffin's A-list living and dining room shows how we used pops of color. The walls are bright white, and one wall in the dining room is covered in Designer's Guild wallpaper. Every single piece of furniture you see has a story—either it was Kathy's and we re-invented it—like her oval dining table that I covered with a giant piece of mirror, or the crazy convex mirror that we joke has a security camera hidden behind it! I had to beg Kathy to trust me on the yellow chairs. She was convinced an old lady had died in them. But their shape is classic and now they're her favorite seats in the house!

This 1970s convex mirror is one-of-a-kind fabulous! It reflects the entire room and plays off the circular theme throughout the house.

$250

The yellow club chairs were covered in bad plaid when I bought them for $45 each at a charity shop. Now they're swinging in chartreuse!

$45

$120

$50

Remember these
roll-down maps
from school?
Who knew
geography could
be so chic?

$50

Trunks make great
industrial-looking
coffee tables and
double as storage.

$20

A signed mid-century lithograph found at a thrift store.

$40

I put a new shade on this mid-century wood and chrome lamp for a clean, mod look.

Map It Out

Do you want one large seating area, like we did in this room, or two smaller congregation points? Try different configurations but be sure to map out exactly what will fit before you go treasure hunting. Don't let a bargain lure you into buying something you don't need. The unexpected mix of found treasures, like the large map and trunk, with new pieces, like the chevron-patterned rug and charcoal gray sofa, create a hip, Bohemian space that totally reflects the personalities of the couple that lives here—sunny, bright, and very fun.

$40

In my friend Lizzie's apartment, these *Mad Men*–style chairs look like a million bucks. The re-covered chairs pick up on the citrus shades in the vintage map of California.

When in doubt, edit out. If you have to think about whether or not you really need to buy something, you probably don't. Same goes when decorating. If you're having doubts, don't do it.

$20

$80

$200

Mid-century sofa from a thrift shop (re-covered in beige linen)

Working Class Wonders

The graphics, shapes, and textures of hard-working industrial pieces from the '30s, '40s, and '50s make amazing, one-of-a-kind art. Look for old signs and industrial workbenches to turn into bars. Metal factory chairs and stools look incredible in a downtown Bohemian space. The vintage sign becomes the focal point in this room. The chrome bookcases house an eclectic mix of flea markets finds. The metal trunk, from a thrift shop, adds an industrial vibe, and the Lucite nesting tables allow the Jonathan Adler rug to shine through.

Mall Chic

I know the term "mall" is not often used in the same sentence as "blue blood." But antique malls get a hall pass. Unlike the giant purveyors of mass-market merchandise that share the same name, antique malls, aka multi-dealer shops, are really just a single roof over the heads of many small, individual shops.

Antique malls work sort of like hair salons. The same way a hairdresser rents a chair at a salon, a dealer rents a booth. There could be as many as a hundred dealers in a center, and each booth has its own personality and mix of merchandise. One booth might be all about French Country, while its next-door neighbor might be Danish Modern through and through. For six years, I sold a mix of English antiques and eclectic accessories at the ivy-covered Antique and Artisan Center in Stamford, Connecticut. Because the rent is lower in an antique mall than paying for an entire storefront, the dealers can afford to pass the savings along to customers. See my Little Black Filofax (page 175) for more information on it and others.

Working the Carpet

There's so much to know about carpets, a person can sometimes—you know—be tempted to just sweep the whole thing under the rug.

The term "Oriental" refers to carpets from Persia, Turkey, India, Russia, and China. I've heard it said that a high-quality carpet can last up to one thousand years—I think fifty to one hundred is a more realistic estimate—and will continue to appreciate in value as it ages. This is because the wool that forms the design is hand-tied to the rug's foundation, so it can't unravel. While there is a huge variation in quality across the spectrum of Oriental rug offerings, some elements that increase price are: hand-spun wools, natural dyes, bright color, rich patina, or unusual design. I don't know about you, but I think a rug looks much better when the hues have mellowed and faded over time. What other people see as tattered, I see as time-worn appeal. Machine-made rugs don't fade like real antique rugs. Rugs are an exception—when it's a good thing to look a

ABOVE: Just one high-quality Oriental rug can take over a year to make! Even at flea markets, dealers can charge in the thousands for a good old carpet. For that reason, many will let you take one home "on approval," to make sure it suits your home.

LEFT: When my friend Megan finds a great old rug that is too frayed for the floor, she cuts it down and sews the remnants into gorgeous, one-of-a-kind throw pillows.

$20

$100

little beaten up. Faded, slightly tattered rugs are a staple in Park Avenue and Greenwich interiors.

At my friend Paulette's Greenwich, Connecticut, home we used classic pieces like the English mahogany chest of drawers, the Georgian chairs, and the nineteenth-century English trunk. This room screams Greenwich Country style, but the zebra-skin pillows add an unexpected twist. I found the folk art portrait at Sotheby's auction gallery. The chest is from an estate sale, and the antique trunk was found at a flea market. Pieces like these can be found at fancy antique stores for thousands more than what I paid.

As soon as I caught a glimpse of this gorgeous Persian carpet in the back of a favorite dealer's van, I knew I had to have it for my friend Paulette's living room—$35 looks like a million!

Chapter 5:
The Gift
of Thrift

Being philanthropic goes hand in hand with being blue-blooded. For aristocrats blessed with good fortune, it is part of the social code to give back. Many choose to do so through giving donations of fine furniture, vintage clothing, jewelry, and accessories to charity thrift shops. Name a cause and there is probably a thrift shop raising money for it. Because these are normally run by a staff of volunteers, with inventory that is given to them, thrift shops aren't greedy about the prices they charge. I love thrift shops because they offer you a twofer. In addition to finding amazing items for your home, you are also helping to fund local and national charities. So you can feel good about going for broke.

Iconic designer and artist Jonathan Adler has called himself a "deranged" thrift shopper. His advice? Keep your eagle eye out for pieces with classic lines, and do your best to ignore the myriad of tragic finishes you will most certainly see. Remember, glossy paint—especially white—is your new best friend.

The Game Plan

Figure out where the New Arrival section of your local thrift shop is, and hit it first. Don't be afraid to ask about when new things come in. While this differs from shop to shop, I have found from my highly unscientific research that Tuesdays and Wednesdays are usually the best days to shop for fresh items. Saturdays tend to be busiest, and Sundays are often picked over.

Ask volunteers or employees for a special events calendar. Most places have additional discount days or events like "the best of the best" at the Jewish Council Thrift Shops in Los Angeles. At this particular event, the most desirable inventory from all over the city is sold at a steep discount. Needless to say, there's always a line.

Get past the tired fabric? Imagine this 1960s sofa in a neutral linen like the sofa below—sweet!

ABOVE: This sleek mid-century sofa is a serious buy for $50. Even if it costs $1,000 to gut and reupholster, you will still spend less than you would at a mid-century antique shop on a comparable piece. Don't forget—at many thrift shops you're recycling and making a cash donation to charity too. Talk about multitasking!

LEFT: This Blakeley sofa, from Jonathan Adler, retails for $3,500. He has built a cottage industry using the sleek shapes of mid-century pieces for his furniture line.

In a new city without much to do? Snag a copy of the local yellow pages and feast your eyes on the section marked "thrift." Every time I go away on assignment for my day job as a TV reporter, I make time to check out the local thrift flavor.

The rules at charity thrift shops are different. No negotiating. If they offer a better price, fantastic. But remember, most thrift shops are set up as charity organizations. All the money they make gets donated. Feel good about spending money you know will go to a good cause.

I lose sight over Lucite pieces like this multipurpose stand. I bought it at a Miami thrift shop for $24, and I think I paid more than that to ship it home! The Hollywood Regency low club chairs were a flea-market find: $60 for the pair. I re-covered them with ten yards of punchy, large-scale floral fabric.

$160

$25

ABOVE: The style of campaign furniture comes from the days of Napoleon, and it has been copied and revered by designers ever since. Furniture with this type of handles and hardware was created so it could be easily moved from one military campaign to another. Apparently, Napoleon liked to live large, even in battle.

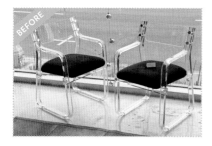

LEFT: Good-bye, plain Janes . . . I followed Jonathan Adler's advice with these faux bamboo, cane-backed armchairs. When I found them, they were more shabby than chic. In glossy white, with new "palm beachy" green fabric, these beauties provide easy-to-move, extra seating in a friend's living room.

$25

$40

Desk Job

This campaign-style desk looked like it belonged in a little boy's room when I bought it for $40, but I saw the potential to go beyond the nursery. When it came to choosing a new paint color, I went with glossy gray—a great alternative to bright white—and had a mirror cut to hide the Formica top. (You can't paint Formica, by the way. I have tried. Trust me.) The desk is luxurious, sparkly, and just great in my master bedroom.

The Lucite chair was also a thrift-shop find: part of a pair for $150. Less than a yard of fabric and a staple gun and she was like new again—but in a fabulous, vintage way. The desk lamps are from Jonathan Adler and the mirror is Z Gallerie.

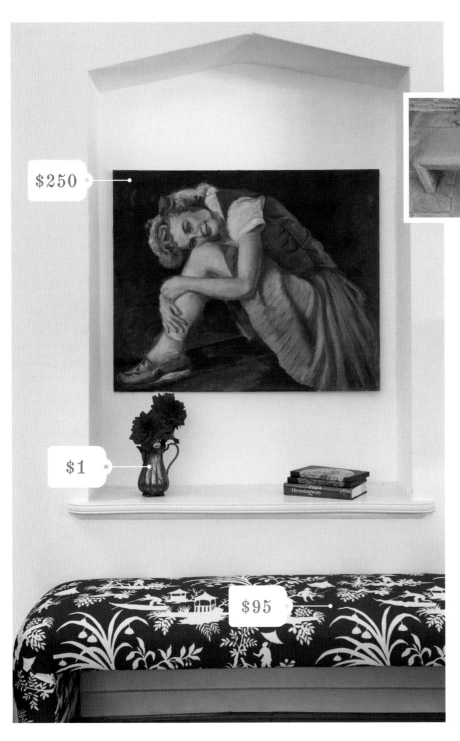

$250

$1

$95

I loved this curvy bench, but not the dusty pink taffeta it was covered in, when I found it for $25 in a thrift shop in L.A. The red chinoiserie fabric adds a classic touch to the mid-century lines. In the end it was a steal for $95.

$20

This macho coffee table base came with a thick piece of glass for $40! Some black glossy paint and it's worthy of being the center of attention in my friend Marnie's chic, Bohemian-style living room.

LEFT: These were lockers from Greenwich Hospital in Connecticut, donated to the thrift shop during a renovation. I bought them for $20 a pair, and my friend Megan had them built into her mudroom to house her boys' sailing gear. Genius!

DESIGN ICON:
Jonathan Adler

I mentioned earlier that no room (or home) should be stuck in any particular design era—the magic is in the mix. I share this philosophy with my design idol, Jonathan Adler, who in addition to being a master potter and interior decorator extraordinaire, shares my obsession with all things secondhand. I asked Mr. Adler to take me along on his time-traveling adventure through this century's decades of design.

LS: Where do you prefer to shop—at thrift shops, flea markets, or sales at private homes?

JA: I'm a flea marketer. During my pretty years, aka my twenties, I was willing to wile away the hours in the most down-and-dirty thrift stores in order to score some incredible trouvés, like lots of groovy Murano glass. But I also had to sort through a lot of unmentionable stuff—some thrift stores even sell used undies, yuck!—and I just can't bring myself to do that anymore. I know this is not a problem for many folks, but to me, house sales can be kind of a bummer sometimes—I just can't help speculating about whatever tragedy befell the house and led to the sale. (Sorry to be such a Debbie Downer!) So, now I prefer the more curated vibe of flea markets. A bit more expensive, but much more efficient.

LS: Which are your favorite decorating styles and periods?

JA: I love the Swinging Sixties, of course! Also, I find Hollywood movies from the fifties totally inspiring—*Pillow Talk*, hello!

LS: What sort of interior design inspires you?

JA: Everything and anything! I'm inspired by designers whose work I admire, such as Gio Ponti, David Hicks, and Bjørn Wiinblad. But I'm also inspired by places such as Capri and India and gorgeous people like Grace Jones, Talitha Getty, and Diana Vreeland. Basically, I just keep my eyes (and my mind) open.

LS: Do you live by a mantra when it comes to thrifting?

JA: If you love it, it will work.

LS: When you hit the flea market, what are you looking for?

JA: I look for unexpected things, bold paintings for instance, or things that come in a series or collection. I've accumulated, and subsequently deaccessioned, so many collections over the years that I'm trying to be more restrained and discriminating in my thrifting these days. I'm afraid I'm not doing a very good job.

LS: Is it humanly possible to put together a great looking room using only finds from house sales, fleas, and thrift shops?

JA: Of course! My pretty years—those long-lost twenties, sigh—were decorated entirely from thrift store finds because secondhand was all I could afford. Even now that I am able to spend more, I still like to mix high and low. Sometimes very expensive furniture can be kinda lugubrious and too precious when it's not balanced by something less serious—and less pricey.

LS: If one can only splurge on one piece in a room, which should it be?

JA: A really comfy sofa with gorgeous fabric.

LS: What do you consider to be the most iconic items of the twentieth century, items that still look fabulous in a wide variety of rooms today?

JA: I'm always on the hunt for a groovy pre-1900 mantique: you know, an antique that's solid and aggressive, not fussy or feminine. Ultimate examples?

I am always on the hunt for vintage Albrizzi.

A hand-carved Gothic mirror or an old trunk.

From the 1950s, I can't get enough Jean Prouvé chairs.

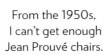

From the 1940s, I've never said no to a chinoiserie shelf by James Mont.

From the 1960s, Warren Platner anything!

A modern couch with clean lines.

I also love anything by Maison Jansen.

Karl Springer did some amazing stuff in the '70s.

One of these things is not like the others . . .

There's one piece in this picture that is very high end. The rest are thrift finds. Care to guess which is which? It's the Chinese Chippendale-style chair, which came from a very high-end boutique. The cowhide seat and original red paint are giveaways to its pedigree, but the thrift shop finds don't look too shabby, do they? The '60s wood-and-chrome lamp and the artwork are equally as stylish, but both came from thrift shops! The amazing geometric lithograph was a true find for $29.99 at a Goodwill. It is signed and numbered by a listed artist. I will explain what that means in a moment.

Imagine where this old metal trunk has been in its travels . . . I wonder who donated it, and what they used it for. Like many of my favorite pieces, it has time-worn appeal—and the orange paint made it a must-have.

I love handmade ceramics like this proud peacock painted in beautiful blues. When I saw the bold signature and incredible craftsmanship, I thought I might have an *Antiques Roadshow* candidate with this 1960s signed ceramic piece. A search in *Davenport's* and on artnet.com showed otherwise. It's strictly a decorative piece by a relatively unknown artist, but I love it regardless. Art is highly individual, and it's what sets a home apart.

Art Attack

I almost had one when I found out my thrift-store Picassos (pictured on the following page) weren't just prints. I bought them because I loved them. I had no idea they were signed or numbered because their mats hid their marks. It wasn't until I had them reframed that I found out my $35 investment was worth thousands.

To research your new acquisitions and give yourself some basic education in the arts, a worthy investment is *Davenport's Art Reference & Price Guide*. It will provide information on hundreds of thousands of "listed" artists ("listed" meaning artists who have actually sold their work). *Davenport's* will tell you how much their works have sold for, and when. It's an invaluable resource—even if you don't find your own set of Picassos.

Visit Artnet.com or Askart.com to see what kind of eye you *really* have!

National Chains: The Starbucks of Philanthropy!

Goodwill is an incredible organization that's been helping people find work since 1902. They have more than 2,400 retail stores, so chances are, there's one near you. In 2009, their retail sales totaled more than $2.4 billion dollars, 83 percent of which went directly to their social programs. There are loads more national organizations with shops all over the place. Use this list to search phone books or search engines.

CHARITY NAME	MISSION
DAV Thrift Stores	Benefiting disabled servicemen since 1920
Deseret Industries	A welfare effort of the Mormon church
Discovery Shops	Supporting the American Cancer Society
ReStores	Benefiting Habitat for Humanity
The Salvation Army	Feeding the hungry
The Society of St. Vincent de Paul	Combating poverty

Picas-so Fabulous!

Yes, you heard me right. Picasso. Picasso, Picasso, Picasso! When I was a reporter at WABC-TV, I used to visit the Salvation Army thrift shop in New York City's Hell's Kitchen with religious devotion. One fateful day, I was rewarded with a pair of authentic, numbered Picasso lithographs for just $35, which have hung in a place of honor in every home I have lived in since.

Authentic, numbered Picasso lithographs for just $35!?

This pair of vintage urn lamps was only $60 at the Elephant's Trunk Flea Market. Robin's-egg blue is one of my favorite accent colors.

I searched "Milo Baughman" on eBay and scored these wood, chrome, and Lucite nightstands for $270. They retail for three times that.

Art Smarts

HERE ARE THE WORDS YOU NEED TO KNOW IN ORDER TO FEEL PERFECTLY COMFORTABLE AT AN ART GALLERY, WHETHER IT'S IN PARIS, SOHO, OR YOUR BASEMENT STORAGE ROOM.

Painting: Yep, you know this one. A one-of-a-kind work, usually on canvas, made with oil, tempera, acrylic, or watercolor paints

Drawing: Also one-of-a-kind, but in pen or pencil, not paint.

Print: One of multiple impressions of a work of art duplicated directly by the artist from his or her own original, made by one of the following processes:

- **Etching:** Acid is used to burn an image into a metallic surface, which is then used as a stamp.

- **Engraving:** Like etching, but with a metal stylus instead of acid.

- **Lithograph:** The artist draws or paints on limestone or metal with a greasy substance, then ink is applied and prints are made.

- **Screen Print, aka Serigraph:** A sheet of thin fabric stretched like a canvas is used as a stencil, and ink is squeegeed across in layers to form the image.

- **Edition Size:** The number of copies made of a reproduced artwork.

In Kathy Griffin's foyer, the star of the show is this Chanel ad by Andy Warhol. The sconces are from JonathanAdler.com, and I had the bench custom made for Kathy to throw her bag on when she comes into the house.

Poster Child

The wild variation in prices on posters can be very confusing. Depending on subject matter and condition, you could pay anywhere from $10 to $10,000. (Get real: We're not talking about my Sean Cassidy posters from second grade.) Posters have become an art field in their own right—but you need to be careful. In order to get what you pay for, make sure you have documentation that your poster is an original, not a reproduction. Check the auction website of Swann Gallery in New York, the ultimate authority on poster art, to hone your eye and get a sense of your poster's value.

In Kathy Griffin's hotel lobby–size entryway, bigger is better. This huge Chanel poster sets the tone for the colors and vibe of the rest of the house. It's one of a set of four I bought on eBay from a gallery in France. Warhol created them for Chanel, for an ad campaign that never ran, sadly, due to his death.

Chapter 6:

A Chip Off the Ol' Block

The auction block, that is.

The three words most of us associate with auctions are, "Going, going, gone!" but don't worry—the auctioneer is not referring to your money! It's incredible finds that are flying out the doors at auction houses, and often the highest bidder isn't bidding very high at all.

Auction houses used to intimidate me. I thought they were all like Sotheby's and Christie's—packed with rich people wearing monocles and smoking jackets—but I couldn't have been more wrong. Auctions are always packed with antique dealers and interior designers for one reason—you can get great pieces for great prices.

Table lamps give off the most flattering light. Leave your overhead lights low and look for chic and unique lamps for every table.

Reserve Judgment

There are thousands of auction houses in the United States, and most people I know are terrified of visiting them. They assume there are no bargains to be had at these hoity-toity establishments, but auctions are actually a great frugalista resource for art, antiques, "recycled" furniture—you name it.

Few people realize that auction houses will often take in the contents of an entire estate so they can get their hands on a few very fine pieces of furniture or art. They will put these pieces into their high-end sales and sell the rest without reserve (meaning whatever it goes for, it goes for) at a general sale.

The Doyle Gallery in New York calls these their "decorator sales"; at Bonhams & Butterfields, they're "estate auctions." There are very nice pieces to be had, but they may not have the provenance or pedigree to make it into one of their premiere auctions. I have scored $3,000 upholstered sofas from Park Avenue apartments for $200.

So while serious collectors and high-end antique dealers are vying for the "important" stuff, you can be getting truly fabulous home furnishings for next to nothing.

(Let's keep this just between us, OK?)

TOP: This woman knows auctions are one of the best places to get great deals on quality antiques, art, and accessories. It's been a trade secret among decorators and dealers for years . . . until now!

BOTTOM: One of my favorite places to spend a lazy Sunday: the charming Braswell Auction House in Norwalk, Connecticut.

When I bought these Staffordshire dog figures, they were just that—figures. I brought them to one of my favorite spots, the Accessory Store in Stamford, who mounted and electrified them. I chose red silk shades rather than white ones for my son Duff's bedroom. Try bringing a pair of just about anything—vases, figurines, old trophies, even musical instruments—to a lighting store to create one-of-a-kind lamps to add personality and twinkle to a room.

ABOVE: The nineteenth-century tobacco figure of a Scottish highlander holds court in my friend Paulette's family room in Greenwich, Connecticut. Mixing in American folk art pieces with shiny black leather wing chairs, a backgammon board, and zebra-striped pillows gave Paulette the clubby look she wanted—without things getting too dark and stuffy. Crisp white paint provides the perfect contrast.

LEFT: Use your auction finds in unexpected ways. I never intended to mount this beautiful nineteenth-century weathervane on a roof when I bought it at Sotheby's Auction House. It's art. Enjoy it, and don't worry about which way the wind blows!

A Fine Mix

Blue-blood style doesn't mean serious or snooty. A room that feels stuffy is not sexy, so add a dash of silliness for good measure. Just like you wouldn't want an entire room done in exclusively French antiques or 100 percent early American decor—break out the powdered wig and hoop skirts—you don't want all the pieces in your home to be from one era, no matter how much you love it. A period room versus a signature one is like comparing costume to fashion.

In addition to mixing eras, I think it's important to mix price points. I like to inject a little high-end elegance into my Dumpster decor. High-quality pieces make the secondhand roses smell better, so to speak. Like the socialite carrying a Chanel bag but wearing her "travel"—aka fake—diamond studs, it's good to keep the focus on the good stuff.

Leslie Keno has been hunting for antiques his whole life, and he appreciates the thrill of a secondhand treasure, especially when it is a great deal. He does suggest splurging on one or two high-quality pieces per room, though, whenever possible. Auctions are great for this because you are still going to get them for less than you would at an antique shop. Remember, auctions are often where antique shops score their inventory. Here are two of my favorite splurges . . .

Where else are you going to find a set of 1940s hand-painted place card holders? Far too fabulous to come out just a couple of times per year, they now hold a place of honor on an equestrian-themed bookshelf.

$75

$150

Art Works!

Auctions are a great place to buy nice paintings that aren't masterpieces commanding major money, but are clearly done by a trained hand. Sometimes they'll be signed, sometimes not. Don't worry about that if you love it. For example, this large oil painting—a 1968 signed still life in gorgeous, muted shades—had a presale estimate of $300–$400. When no one else bid, I scored it for a friend's guest room for only $75. That's the magic of "no reserve" auctions!! If there had been a reserve placed on the piece, it would have been passed—not sold—and it would have been put up for sale again at a later date or returned to its original owner. It's one-of-a-kind chic for the price of a mass-produced knockoff. Now *that's* blue-blood style on a blue-collar budget!

Hammer Time

The "wonder twins" of *Antiques Roadshow*, Leigh and Leslie Keno, are both preeminent authorities when it comes to American antiques. They also know their way around an auction gallery. Leslie is the senior VP of furniture for Sotheby's; Leigh runs his own auction house, Keno Auctions. Both have been buying and selling at auctions since they were young boys. Below they answer some questions on becoming a bidder.

LARA: How does one find out about local auctions?

LESLIE: Two of my favorite resources are *Maine Antiques Digest* and *Antiques and the Arts Weekly*. You can subscribe to these trade papers and both have websites [see my Little Black Filofax on page 173]. I also like Artfact.com because you can watch auctions real-time and bid online.

LARA: But if I bid online or by phone, I can't look over the item to make sure it is in good condition. Is that safe?

LEIGH: Yes. You can call the auction house and ask for a full condition report on anything you are interested in bidding on. Most auction websites will also post several pictures of each item in their online catalog and will guarantee them to be as described. If the item is worth a lot, you may want to hire an expert to inspect and bid for you. Most reputable dealers will do this for a percentage of the hammer price (the last and winning bid when the hammer goes down). You can also do a "left bid," which is when you write down the top amount you are willing to pay, and if no one bids above it, you win. But you should never bid unless you do your homework.

LESLIE: At Sotheby's you can always call and speak to one of our specialists. We are always available to answer questions.

LARA: A lot of people aren't aware of the "buyer's premium."

LESLIE: This is the fee the auction house charges to the buyer. It can range from 12 to 25 percent of the final price of an item. The auction house also charges a seller's premium—usually the same percentage, if at some point you decide to sell an item through them. Check the auction house's website or call to find out what the auction house charges so you are not surprised at checkout.

LARA: A lot of auction houses offer free appraisal days. Can you explain how that works?

LEIGH: Many auction houses, including Keno Auctions, offer free appraisals. Bring in your piece or e-mail pictures for information on its value. Many people do this and then consign the item to be sold in an upcoming auction.

BITE ME.

Add chrome tacks to
a plain headboard to
give it a little zing!

Our blue-blooded friend the monogram
pops up again. The simple addition of
the purple embroidery to the bedspread
ties the look together in a chic,
personal way.

KHP

Lavender and pink? Why not? I combined pink accents with lavender geometric wallpaper, a cheeky painting by L.A. pop artist Todd Goldman, and a custom headboard with a chrome-tack Greek key pattern for a zany, happy boudoir fit for a modern princess of any age.

Don't take this whole decorating thing too seriously. Figure out what makes you happy and go for it.

No Backsies

A final and very important lesson about auctions: Once you've bid, you're in the game. So make sure you factor in the buyer's premium and understand this: If you raise your paddle, whether in cyberspace or on the auction floor, and the hammer goes down, the old "I was just waving to a friend across the room" trick isn't going to fly. Put on your big-girl panties and pay up!

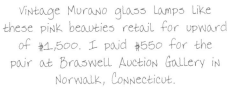

Vintage Murano glass lamps like these pink beauties retail for upward of $1,500. I paid $550 for the pair at Braswell Auction Gallery in Norwalk, Connecticut.

Chapter 7:
A Web of Buys

I've always just loved how, in old movies, all a socialite has to do is ring a silver bell and, as if by magic, whatever she fancies at that moment just appears in front of her: afternoon tea, wardrobe options, a pet tiger—anything she desires. This is how I view the Web.

I mean, what could be better—or more dangerous, for those of us with a slight shopping problem—than having twenty-four-hour access to secondhand shopping? A person can decorate an entire room without getting out of her bed. Sites such as eBay, 1st Dibs, and One Kings Lane allow an armchair decorator to browse, buy, or research just about any treasure she could ever imagine, all on her own time.

Keep It Real

The best way to shop the Web is to also shop the real world. I like to browse shops and multidealer centers and jot down descriptions of pieces I like. Before I even consider pulling out my wallet, I break out the laptop and see if I can find it online for less.

That's how I found Warren Platner nickel wire lounge chairs I had long coveted. They cost a small fortune at a shop that specialized in mid-century design, so I decided to take my hunt to the Web.

When I first typed "Platner chairs" into the search engine, all that came up were bad knockoffs. But on my tenth try—remember, persistence is everything!—*eureka*! I struck interior design gold. Someone in Atlanta had just listed a pair on eBay, offering a buy-it-now price of less than half of what the shop was charging.

Ship Shape

You may be thinking, "How did she ship all this stuff? It must have cost a fortune!" Two words: seller's problem. As the buyer, you pay shipping costs—be sure to check their methods and calculations carefully so you know what you are signing up for—but the seller is the one who needs to figure out how to get their wares to your front door. I have been to the Greyhound bus station more times than I care to mention, to pick up boxes of finds (cheap travel means cheap shipping). Many sellers offer delivery by way of bus, which means you do have to go to your local depot to pick up your purchase. In fact, the ceramic greyhound in the image at right was delivered via Greyhound. Ironic, no?

The faience pottery greyhound was a 1stdibs.com find. (You can also search for "whippets" if you're looking for these online.)

My husband's "toy" is losing the battle against my finds, which have taken over the garage as I reinvent them for a new project. You call it hoarding? I call it heaven!

Not only were these authentic Platner chairs, but they were also the larger size that has become nearly impossible to find. I replaced the worn fabric with deep eggplant mohair because it is durable yet looks and feels luxurious.

Surfin' USA

BELOW ARE SOME OF MY FAVORITE PLACES TO SHOP ONLINE.

EBAY.com Register and bid in online auctions or use the buy-it-now function for immediate gratification. Remember that on eBay you are only as good as your "feedback" score. If you are the winning bidder and reneg, or don't pay promptly, the seller will leave you negative feedback. Many people won't allow those with negative feedback to bid. Same goes for the seller, though. If you aren't happy and leave a seller negative feedback, buyers will not trust them anymore. A giant honor system self-polices the eBay community. Make sure you check a seller's feedback before you bid, and leave positive feedback if you have a good experience. eBay is a great resource for both secondhand furnishings and brand-new fixtures. Manufacturers are now using eBay to sell overstocked items and leftovers. I got the Restoration Hardware–style vanity in my powder room for $350. An almost identical one sells on restorationhardware.com for $3,000!

1stDibs.com A high-end portal that showcases the wares of fine antiques shops and dealers from all over the country. Definitely more expensive, but well worth visiting, 1stdibs is a cyber showplace of eye candy for your house. I have purchased pieces through this site, but I also use it all the time for research and ideas.

ETSY.com Etsy started as a community site where crafters could sell their handmade wares, but it has quickly morphed into a hipster mini-mall with an excellent selection of home decor. Whether you're looking for a fiberglass Eames office chair or a set of 1970s needlepoint pillows, you're likely to find it—or something just as unusual—on Etsy. To bypass the craft and clothing options and go direct to home decor, just type www.etsy.com/category/vintage/furniture into your browser.

ThisIsNotIkea.com (This Is Not Ikea) My friend Alexis and his partners came up with this website as a place to sell their L.A. yard-sale and thrift-shop finds. If you can't fly here and go "sale-ing" with me, this site is the next best thing. Set designers, interior decorators, and this girl love the industrial furniture and quirky pop art Alexis offers. If you are looking for a well-traveled, Bohemian vibe but haven't really been anywhere—this is one trip you need to make.

Peek into my Little Black Filofax on page 173 for some more of my must-visit sites. Prepare to be inspired.

When you buy vintage lighting be sure to check the wiring. If it looks even a little iffy, have it rewired.

Lighting Is the Jewelry of the House

Just like a great pair of earrings can complete your outfit, sconces and chandeliers add a little sparkle to your home. The Verner Panton ceiling fixture in my powder room, an eBay find, is made of dozens of smoky Murano glass squares.

From years of being on TV, I know that lighting is everything. No one looks good when lit from directly above, so don't rely on overhead lighting, unless it's a gorgeous, over-the-top chandelier on a dimmer. Table and floor lamps offer a much more flattering glow.

$10

$20

eBay?

MARTINI

$10

$2

$5

THIS PAGE: This Mies van der Rohe Barcelona daybed, Arco light, and Sputnik chandelier can all be had with the click of your mouse—and some credit card info, of course. The chartreuse paint adds punch to an otherwise neutral palette. The Greek key rug provides texture and pattern galore.

OPPOSITE TOP: Kathy can fit all ten chairs comfortably around her dining table, but normally keeps it down to eight so the room doesn't look too crowded.

OPPOSITE BOTTOM: I found this office waiting-room bench, formerly covered in hideous burnt-orange vinyl, at thisisnotikea.com. It provides a groovy place to cop a squat and enjoy the view at Kathy's house.

INSIDER TIP

Paint or wallpaper one wall— it's a small commitment and makes a big impact.

Search eBay for vintage scarves like this one by Hermès. Framed, the horsey motif makes a fashionable statement as wall art.

THIS PAGE: Little rooms don't need little furniture! The bigger the pieces are, the bigger the space looks. The Victorian walnut buffet with mirrored doors was only $200 at an auction, and the early nineteenth-century side chair was an estate sale find from Rhode Island.

OPPOSITE: Both the zebra-print fabric (1980s deadstock) and the shag poufs came from eBay. I am way into poufs right now—I love how much fun it is just to say the word "pouf," and how handy they are to have around for company. The Studio 54 vibe was inspired by this glamorous picture of my friend Rebecca's mom. She blew it up at Kinko's for less than $10 and voilà—a personalized "Warhol"!

Getting Personal

By putting my husband's family name into the search box, we have been able to assemble an amazing collection that is near and dear to our hearts. David's great-grandfather started a brewery in the late 1800s that stayed in the family until the 1960s. eBay finds like this pre-Prohibition serving tray are more than cool wall art. They're pieces of family history that will surely become treasured heirlooms. Sounds very blue blood until you see the beer can collection in my husband's office.

In-Sites

Sure, Edison said that genius is 1 percent inspiration and 99 percent perspiration, but that 1 percent means the world to the decor-obsessed like me. As such, the Web isn't just a great place to shop—it's also a great place to discover new ideas and hone your aesthetic. Here are just a few of the sites I visit when I need to get out of my own head. You'll find a longer list of resources in the back of this book.

TheParisApartment.com
For a whimsical yet sophisticated European vintage feel

MaineAntiquesDigest.com
As suggested by the genius Keno brothers—a geeky (in the best way) antiques resource

ApartmentTherapy.com
A network of linked local sites that display the innovative interiors of users, as well as announce exclusive deals and offer a great community of other decor-obsessed people

Designwatcher.blogspot.com
A smart, quirky, ahead-of-the-curve style journal about living a great-looking life

Notcot.org
A weird collection of innovations and obsessions

Life.com
This legendary magazine has an incredible archive of iconic photos that will inspire endlessly

Lonnymag.com
Founded by former editors at *Domino*, my number-one favorite, tragically defunct home decor bible, this site simulates the mag experience with actual pages to flip

DesignWithinReach.com
A virtual catalog of authorized reproductions of classic modern furniture. A great place to learn shapes and names

Try punching in these iconic designers:

SAARINEN   CHERNER

EAMES   JAMES MONT

PLATNER

Try searching for these key terms to find decadent decor:

GREEK KEY   FAUX BAMBOO

LUCITE   CHINESE CHIPPENDALE

MID-CENTURY

CHROME

The Five Requirements

Just like a proper lady, a piece of furniture should be refined to near perfection. And the best examples of femininity and decor have the same qualities in common.

Charm

She has a signature appeal all her own.

Style

She knows how to express herself to her own best advantage.

Dress Code

She knows how to present herself.

Balance

She stands on her own two feet—and looks damn good doing it.

Sociability

She plays well with others.

Chapter 8:
Refinishing School

Finishing school is where a young lady goes to ensure she is polished, elegant, and ready to be presented to the world. If it was good enough for Lady Diana, it's good enough for your soon-to-be-fabulous furniture. For your diamonds in the rough, refinishing school means restoration, paint, reupholstery, and sometimes a little creative thinking.

~Re-Finishing School~

certifies that
Your Fabulous Find
has hereby completed the necessary
requirements to officially go
from trash to treasure
Diploma
Tara Spencer

Graffiti Artist

Spray paint isn't just for tagging the sides of buildings anymore. Home Depot, Lowe's, and even your local hardware store carry a myriad of colors and finishes for your do-it-yourself moment. Just follow Mark's directions on page 143—and don't be scared of a little bit of color.

Don't Be a Hero

SOME PIECES SIMPLY REQUIRE A PROFESSIONAL'S HELP.

Full Disclosure: I am no Martha Stewart. As Kenny Rogers once crooned, "You've got to know when to hold 'em, know when to fold 'em."

In the case of refinishing pieces, I can staple and spray paint with the best of 'em—but if something is really big or potentially really fabulous, I am all about leaving it to the experts. I figure I'm saving so much on the furniture, it's often worth paying to ensure the piece will end up looking perfect. Most handymen or restoration experts will paint a piece—like the coffee table whose big reveal you're about to see on page 140—for about $100.

Did I mention I paid $5 for it at an estate sale?

1. Good bones! Remember?

2. I loved the hardware but not the blah beige when I bought it for $79! The vintage Drexel buffet was hardly a standout when I snatched it up at a Goodwill store.

3. Painter Rick Sanchez applies the coral red high-gloss paint with a spray gun for a flawless finish.

4. In glossy paint with polished pulls, the buffet now takes center stage. Not bad for a $79 Goodwill charity case.

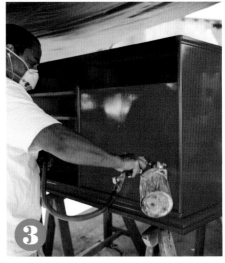

Here's another one of the Warhol Chanel ads I bought on eBay.

N°5
CHANEL

CHANEL

The showstopper is flanked by two faux bamboo hall chairs I found at the Rose Bowl for only $40 each.

$40

$79

Reupholstering took these from worn out to white hot!

After a good scrub and sanding, my painter applied primer and several coats of paint. For a super-glossy finish, he buffs between coats.

Social climber? With a coat of red paint on the legs, this old ladder makes a great bohemian bookshelf!

Like a gal in a little black dress, this formerly frumpy coffee table looks sleek and chic! Mixed in with high-end furniture and other flea-market finds, you'd never know she was a castoff!

Painting 101

If I have a master's degree from this make-believe refinishing school, Mark Devito has his PhD. He runs a family business, Raphael's Furniture Restoration in Stamford, Connecticut, which was founded in the 1960s by his dad, and is the go-to guy for New York and Connecticut antiques dealers and retail customers alike—including yours truly! Below, Mark offers some tips, a cheat sheet if you will, for refining your time-worn finds.

Here are his tips on painting:

- Make sure the piece you're thinking about painting isn't a period antique. If you are even a little unsure about its history, do not clean the finish until you have an expert look at it. You could be wiping away thousands of dollars.

- Proper cleaning is crucial to ensure a lasting finish—and believe it or not, good old Windex does an excellent job.

- Use superfine "0000" steel wool or 220-grit sandpaper to rough up the surface of wood.

- Always prime before painting.

- Wondering what kind of paint to use? On raw wood, use oil-based paint: It is most durable—the glossier, the better!

- If the wood has been lacquered or painted before, use the same type of paint it's accustomed to: latex over latex, water based over water based.

- On metal, Rust-Oleum is a great choice.

- Use several coats of paint, whether you're applying with a brush or spraying on. Let the piece dry, go over it with steel wool to buff, and apply another coat. Three to four coats usually does the trick.

- For a super-glossy look, do one last buff when your last coat of paint dries, then finish with an even coat of clear gloss lacquer.

What Can Brown Do for You?

It's a lot more work than painting a piece, but stained wood pieces can be elegant and clubby. According to Mark:

Paint thinner will remove an existing finish.

Apply stain to the naked wood in several coats to get the depth and color you want. (I like mahogany and walnut tones that don't have a lot of red in them.)

Finish with glossy clear lacquer spray. Varnish, shellac, or tongue oil are all alternatives for the top coat.

Here's the most important lesson: Whatever you choose, do it in a well-ventilated area with your hands and face covered. (My mom used to set up shop in our garage, with all the doors up to let the fresh air in.)

#20 apiece at a garage sale?

THIS PAGE: This white elephant is way too cool to sweep under the rug. The one-of-a-kind vintage bar came out of a Palm Beach estate. The split reed club chairs were in pretty bad shape, which is why I got them for such a steal. New cushions done in a Sunbrella geometric fabric and glossy white spray change everything.

OPPOSITE: Mahogany can be a little bit mundane. A can of Rust-Oleum Painter's Touch Ultra Cover 2x in Berry Pink transformed the boring brown mirror frame to fantastic fuchsia!

Nice (Auto) Body!

THE MAGICAL ART OF POWDER COATING

Powder coating will give your metal furniture a paint job worthy of a Porsche. In fact, it's the exact process used to give cars their perfectly smooth shiny finish in any color you can imagine. Most auto painters will also paint your metal pieces, so just ask! It can be pricey but the result is flawless. Just like your car, your patio set can live outside year-round without risk of rusting.

Do Not Try This at Home

At Steel Santos, a refinishing shop in Los Angeles, each piece is hung on a hook and painted as it moves along a track. The pieces are first sandblasted to remove any old paint and then sprayed with compressed air to remove dust. Then they pass through a 400 degree oven where the paint adheres to the metal. The result? See for yourself.

These would be great powder coated!

These old sneaker lockers were abandoned by a high school and adopted by me at the Long Beach Flea Market. I had just the baskets powder coated in high-gloss white. By keeping the frame the original metal finish, the look is still industrial in my son Duff's room. The big framed monopoly cards were $10 each at a thrift shop.

TITLE DEED
BOARDWALK

RENT $50.

With 1 House	$ 200.
With 2 Houses	600.
With 3 Houses	1400.
With 4 Houses	1700.

With HOTEL $2000.

Mortgage Value $200.
Houses cost $200. each
Hotels, $200. plus 4 houses

If a player owns ALL the Lots of any Color-Group, the rent is Doubled on Unimproved Lots in that group.

TITLE DEED
PARK PLACE

RENT $35.

With 1 House	$ 175.
With 2 Houses	500.
With 3 Houses	1100.
With 4 Houses	1300.

With HOTEL $1500.

Mortgage Value $175.
Houses cost $200. each
Hotels, $200. plus 4 houses

If a player owns ALL the Lots of any Color-Group, the rent is Doubled on Unimproved Lots in that group.

These are vintage, made by Milton Bradley, but you could make them using a color printer!

Steel Santos sells a rainbow of powder-coated pieces at the Rose Bowl every month.

Dozens of people walked past this vintage outdoor table and chairs before I snapped them up at an estate sale for just $150. Powder-coated robin's-egg blue, it's my favorite perch for morning coffee or sunset wine.

These faux bamboo-style metal chairs had a great look but were rusty from sitting outside unprotected. Powder-coated a sunny shade of citrine, they brighten up the patio year-round.

The Charlie Chaplin movie poster—an original—and most of the other accessories for the bookshelves came from a center in Connecticut.

Snazzy Dresser

A little pull can get you into the best restaurant at a moment's notice—and it can be all your dresser needs to go from drab to fab. Never be content with the knobs that come with it—be discerning and choose the ones that seem just right to you.

The Big Cover-Up

Having your clothing custom made is the ultimate upper-crust luxury. The fabric hugs all the right curves, is lean where it needs to be, and is forgiving when called for. Reupholstering is the same thing, and nothing breathes new life into an old piece more than a great reupholstery job.

If your piece has been around the block one too many times, she may need a new filling, and on sofas, there is nothing like down feathers to flop onto. According to *Country Living* magazine, the average cost of labor for re-covering a standard sofa is about $350. Larger sofas will cost more, as will changing the filling. Love seats and chairs will be less. Make sure you get a quote and shop around. Word of mouth has always landed me great workers, so ask around. I can tell you the prices are higher in Los Angeles and Connecticut, but again, you are getting a custom sofa for significantly less than you'd pay at a retail store. You are recycling a one-of-a-kind frame that will set your room apart. The fabric is also an additional cost to consider. See the chart on the next page for an idea of how many yards you will need.

These are estimates using solid fabric. If your fabric has a pattern, in order to match, it will take slightly more.

My Martha moment: Re-covering a simple cushion is easy. Use a staple gun and start in the middle of one side, pulling super tight as you work your way out on each side. Fold the corners like a Christmas present!

standard-width 80-inch sofa	15 yards
small club chair	4 yards
wing chair	8 yards
dining chair (seat cushion only)	1/2 yard

What to Wear

You must take as much care choosing fabrics in which to dress your finds as
you would seeking an outfit you had to wear 365 days a year. I think being
called "timeless," whether you're a woman, a handbag, a sofa, or a song, is just
about the greatest compliment there is.

When reinventing your flea-market finds, you must make refurbishing
choices that will last a lifetime—both literally and figuratively. Nowhere is
timelessness more important than fabric. (Watch a couple of low-budget
1970s movies and you'll know just what I mean.)

In downtown Los Angeles, there are countless fabric stores with hugely
discounted prices. I will share some of my favorites in my Little Black Filofax
(page 173).

The Raw Materials

LEARN THE NAMES OF THESE WEAVES; THEY'LL BE AROUND FOREVER,
AND THEY'LL NEVER GO OUT OF STYLE

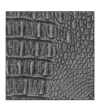

Chinoiserie: Asian-inspired, elegant, and playful—go crazy and do an entire room, or just a couple of accent pillows. From Palm Beach to Park Ave, this type of print is eternally chic and versatile.

Ikat (pronounced "ee-kat"): The word ikat means "to bind." An ancient way of dying fabric created in Asia. Very popular pattern seen in all types of interiors.

Faux Leather: Durable beyond words, this fancy plastic—aka "vinyl"—looks chicest when embossed with a crocodile or ostrich pattern, for richness and texture. Great for chairs because it's virtually impossible to ruin.

Animal Prints: Cheetah, leopard, and zebra have become designers' go-to "neutrals." They complement many styles and These work in both modern and traditional rooms. Leopard- or zebra-print rugs are a designer favorite for adding texture and movement to a space.

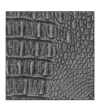

Flame Stitch: This traditional pattern has made a resurgence in more transitional interiors. Comes from a needlepoint stitch that produces a pattern resembling flames.

Chevron Stripe: The chevron stripe can be seen in ancient heralding, military badges, and most famously in Charlie Brown's iconic yellow shirt. Designers love this zigzag pattern for rugs and upholstery to add modern zing to any room.

Geometrics: Masculine or feminine, depending on color scheme and scale, they look right at home in a modern space or can add zip to a more traditional look. David Hicks made the pattern famous, now it's available almost anywhere.

Chintz: There's nothing chintzy about the florals made popular in English country interiors. Just ask designer Mario Buatta, nicknamed the Prince of Chintz.

CHINTZ Happens!

WILLIAM NORWICH

Be Inventive

Sometimes even the best-bred must be willing to flout convention. I snagged this piece of decorative woodwork directly from our very own Dumpster during the renovation of our L.A. home. Although originally meant to "live" on the home's exterior, I thought it had great potential as a dramatic interior backdrop. I gave the two pieces of woodwork a fresh coat of paint and a set of hinges, and fashioned a sturdy mid-century screen that adds definition to a reading nook.

In the next sections, I'll show you loads more marvelous makeovers—and the incredible way they come together in finished rooms.

1. The house we bought had these geometric wood screens covering two windows.

2. During the renovation, the contractors threw them in the Dumpster. I think not!

3. Simple hinges from the hardware store will allow the panels to stand on their own. A fresh coat of paint and they are transformed into a '60s-style screen.

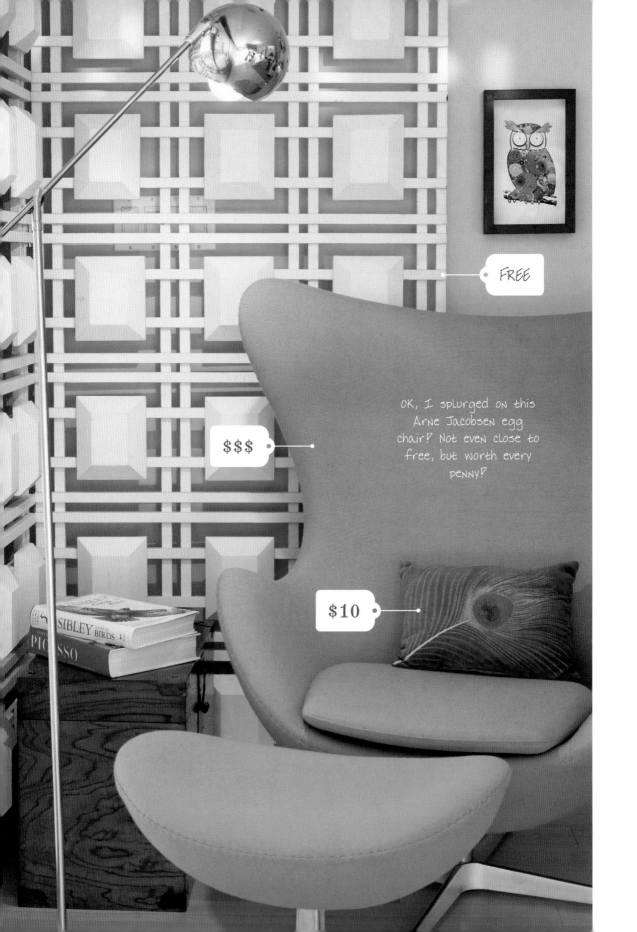

Chapter 9:
From Duckling to Swan

Who doesn't love a good makeover? From Audrey Hepburn in *My Fair Lady* to Oprah giving real house-wives the Hollywood starlet treatment, there is nothing better than watching a duckling emerge as a swan.

Hopefully, this chapter will change the way you look at things the next time you hit the circuit. The saying "Don't judge a book by its cover" is about to take on a whole new meaning.

$50 for the crab lamp at an estate sale didn't pinch my wallet!

Faux bamboo is timeless and works in mid-century, Hollywood regency, and more traditional rooms as well. This mirror was a major score that just needed a new home to shine again.

This vintage Baker dresser had the right bones but the wrong paint job. It's a classic that deserves to be in classic colors like white and blue. Paint remover revealed shiny brass pulls. The crab lamp looked crusty when I bought it with a dull ivory shade that overwhelmed it. Now? Two claws up! The 1930s boxing trophy that doubles as a vase adds a sporty touch.

My daugter Kate saw this and immediately thought it would make a great night-light. A lightbulb moment indeed!

It could make a smashing chandelier too—an easy project for a handyman or electrician.

Having a second job is not normally the blue-blood way, but lots of pieces do double-duty beautifully. When does the caged bird sing? When you turn its antiquated birdcage into a lighting fixture! Who keeps parakeets anymore, anyway?

Palm Springs, Full Swing

Another piece with a double life? Kathy's coffee table is actually a nineteenth-century turned-wood child's bed I found at a thrift store. I made it new with a thick piece of glass on top. The size of the child's bed frame was the perfect scale for the sofas. The charcoal gray shag rug is from eBay. Something you'll notice in all the rooms in this book? I try to keep the same color theme running though a house, even if it's only with a couple of accessories, to create visual continuity.

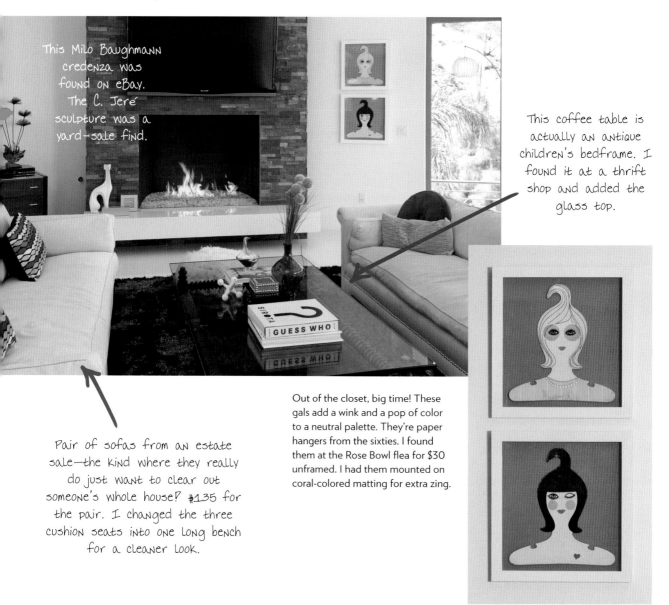

This Milo Baughmann credenza was found on eBay. The C. Jeré sculpture was a yard-sale find.

This coffee table is actually an antique children's bedframe. I found it at a thrift shop and added the glass top.

Pair of sofas from an estate sale—the kind where they really do just want to clear out someone's whole house? $135 for the pair. I changed the three cushion seats into one long bench for a cleaner look.

Out of the closet, big time! These gals add a wink and a pop of color to a neutral palette. They're paper hangers from the sixties. I found them at the Rose Bowl flea for $30 unframed. I had them mounted on coral-colored matting for extra zing.

STYLE *is* **KNOWING** *who you are, what you want* **TO SAY,** *and not giving a* **DAMN.**

GORE VIDAL

It's a Mass-terpiece!

I know I talk a lot about one–of-a-kind pieces, but sometimes it is impossible to find exactly what you need. For this, I have found some big chain stores to be a huge resource. Great designers like Thomas O'Brien, Victoria Hagan, John Derian, and Jonathan Adler have all created lines for Target, for goodness' sake—we might as well take advantage of them!

Besides Target, you should browse the stores or websites of the following: CB2, West Elm, Home Goods, Ikea, and Pier 1. Also hit stores like Home Depot for all of the tools of the trade—spray paint, stain, and steel wool are just a few of the staples in my bag of tricks.

I love plant stands with Boston ferns cascading over them! The faux bamboo stands were just $20 at the Council Thrift Shop in Los Angeles!

These were old and crusty, but just look at 'em now!

Shell Shock

My friend Rebecca almost walked right by these grotto chairs, but boy are we glad she didn't. At $500, she thought they were expensive at the Huntington Collection Retail Thrift Shop in Pasadena. (See my Little Black Filofax on page 173 for details.) Not only are they a wow in white, we also found the exact same set on 1stdibs.com for $5,800!!

INSIDER TIP

No fake plants, please. Ever.

Best Chest

Painting this chest black was not an obvious choice; after all, the wood finish is classic. But the dark shine contrasts brilliantly with the brass hardware and adds a chic modern element to a traditional piece. And these barrel-backed chairs may have started out as yard-sale orphans, but now they feel right at home in a Park Avenue pad!

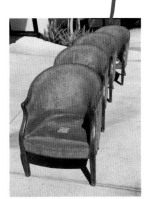

This little guy was pretty beaten up with scratches and dings, but still way too cute to pass up for $40. Now he's all man!

A Harmonious Mix

The mahogany lyre-back chair (opposite) was in perfect condition and already covered in a chic animal print fabric when I spotted it at the Long Beach Flea Market for a price of $50. The nineteenth-century English chest and carved faux bamboo mirror were both estate sale finds. A Park Avenue look on a Main Street budget. Music to my ears.

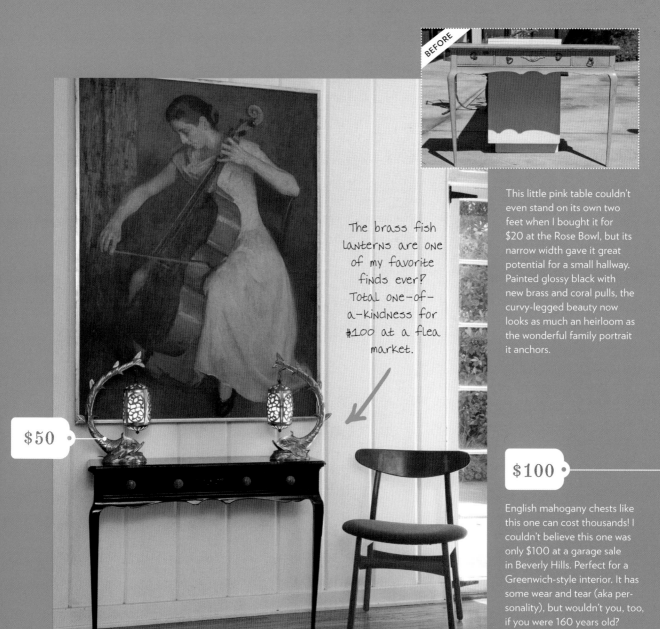

BEFORE

The brass fish lanterns are one of my favorite finds ever! Total one-of-a-kindness for #100 at a flea market.

This little pink table couldn't even stand on its own two feet when I bought it for $20 at the Rose Bowl, but its narrow width gave it great potential for a small hallway. Painted glossy black with new brass and coral pulls, the curvy-legged beauty now looks as much an heirloom as the wonderful family portrait it anchors.

$50

$100

English mahogany chests like this one can cost thousands! I couldn't believe this one was only $100 at a garage sale in Beverly Hills. Perfect for a Greenwich-style interior. It has some wear and tear (aka personality), but wouldn't you, too, if you were 160 years old?

$20

I found these already framed on velvet at a thrift shop and grouped on a wall. They are classic, but the white circular shape of the medallions feel modern at the same time.

$50

How great is this musical chair? Hard to believe it was a flea find. You're such a Lyre? Nope, I'm not?

Putting It All Together

So you know what to buy and where to buy it. You know how to make it over, and how to make it up. Now what?

Like fresh-faced first years packing up for boarding school, it's finally time for you to express yourselves! I've included strategies for combining, organizing, and styling your thrift scores. But the rest, as they say, is up to you.

High art? Coromandel screen? Nope. It's framed wallpaper! (I can take 'em with me when I move!)

INSIDER TIP

Find a signature shade that can run throughout your home to provide continuity—even if only with small accessories.

Much better
in white faux
leather?

Double Take

As I find pieces, I tend to redecorate. Sometimes in the middle of the night. Here's my LA living room with a huge circular rug I found in Palm Springs. The 1950s lounge chair looked like it belonged in a dentist's office, but it is beyond comfy and I love the kitsch factor. Peacock feathers are a fun alternative to fresh flowers (and last longer too!). The "vase" is actually a groovy umbrella stand.

The lamps? Goodwill, for less than $10 each?

Eighteenth-century Lithographs for $10 each? Gotta love a good garage sale.

BEFORE

It really doesn't look like the same couch, does it? Oh how I love a single seat cushion. $160, UCLA Thrift Shop.

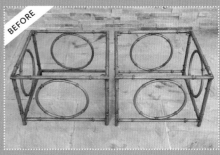

BEFORE

Not sure this bucket would do much to put out a fire, but I loved the old red paint and lettering. $5 at a thrift shop!

Nineteenth-century campaign chest, $500 at a multidealer shop. Pricey, I know—but it's an antique. Now, it's an heirloom!

BEFORE

Found these armchairs on eBay! I'm mad for plaid on their clubby, curvy lines.

Better off red, right? I mean, they did come from the Rose Bowl.

Cool Ikat

Treasures found in my down-and-dirty haunts can go uptown pretty easily. Conversely, if I had covered the chairs and sofa in white, painted the cocktail tables glossy black, and used a geometric pattern instead of ikat pillows, the room would have a very different feel.

Mixed Doubles

When a couple moves in together, finding a style that represents them both, yet doesn't look like a hodgepodge, can be a challenge. This room aces it.

I love the contrast between the glitz and glamour of the chandelier, and the whimsy and athleticism of the oversized tennis racket. Ditto the contrast between the bike and the unusual art piece, which evokes softness and nature. The couple fell in love with this lithograph at an atelier in Paris. It's the room's major splurge.

The young couple was able to get an amazing deal on these authentic Modernica chairs by ordering them online, saving tax and getting free shipping.

The beach cruiser, which is a contemporary design by Paul Frank, retails for more than $400, but they were able to find a barely used one on Craigslist for just $100.

What a racquet? This was an advertising display from the '70s. I paid $50 for it at a flea market. You can find just about anything supersized at thinkbig.com.

The dining room was put together with pieces from the Web, flea markets, thrift shops, and high-end shops to create a mid-century meets Hollywood Regency party.

The octagonal mirror was naked pine when I bought it at a thrift store. Now it's a sophisticated glossy black.

These Russell Woodard chairs were shipped via Greyhound bus after I bought them on eBay!

This campaign-style chest was just $40! I put some spring back in its step by painting the worn-out white a glossy kelly green.

The groovy green and gold 60s vases were just $5 for the pair!

A mass—terpiece from
Low-price furniture
website zgallerie.com.

$300

$100

$37

Secondhand Symmetry

I am all about mixing low- and high-end, and ide-
ally you can do that. But I just had to show you
how you really can use pieces from *just* the places
on my "circuit." This room is almost 100 percent
secondhand style. From the chrome étagères to
the rug—even the wallpaper came from one of my
now not-so-secret sources. I grabbed pieces you
have seen in other settings to show you how things
can be moved around and work just as well . . .
and sometimes even better. So experiment! Move
things around. There are a million ways to skin a
cat—and almost as many different ways to set up
your space.

Le Corbusier daybeds have been stylish for
over forty years and will still be in another forty.
This is the kind of piece I always recommend buying. The chrome étagères I got at a Connecticut
auction were such a steal, even the shipping cost
to Los Angeles didn't make me think twice. The
wool sisal rug and grass cloth wallpaper were both
factory closeouts on eBay, and while I am still not
over that sunburst mirror I should have bought at
the Rose Bowl, this one definitely dulls the pain.
The shelves of the étagère are filled with pieces I
have collected in my travels, and also games for
the kids. Because this *is* real life, after all.

I put this room together as an
experiment. I wanted to prove
that even while on a blue-collar
budget, you can achieve blue-
blood style. Every single piece
here, except for the mirror, is a
found treasure. Aren't you dying
to start hunting for yourself?

I am now about to say to you the two words my ears are always longing to hear:

Go shopping.

It's time! You're ready! You'll want this book with you—especially the section you're about to read.

I call it my Little Black Filofax because it just sounds much more stylish than a Black-Berry, no? In my Little Black Filofax, you'll find the contact information for some of my favorite people, places, and resources. I hope they help you as much they have helped me.

Some final thoughts as you head out: Don't take your décor too seriously. I know there are rules and guidelines that help achieve an awesome interior; I agree that scale, symmetry, and the mix of pieces are all important. And yes, there are things I strongly suggest you should not do (such as display a Beanie Baby collection on your mantel), but rules are made to be broken (just ask my grade-school teachers). The most important lesson my mom has taught me? Have fun! Buy things that make you smile. Your home is your refuge. So make it uniquely *you*. I hope you've gotten some ideas, inspiration, and valuable information during our time together. Come back and refer to this book whenever you need to. Sticky notes are welcome if you want to mark something you really like!

Now may the benevolent bargain gods smile upon thee, and remember— a true hunter knows it is as much about the pursuit as actually bagging the prize.

xoxo,
Lara

Little Black Filofax

CALIFORNIA

Alameda Point Antiques and Collectibles Faire
2900 Navy Way
Alameda, California 94501
510-522-7500
alamedapointantiquesfaire.com

A. N. Abell Auction Company
Great treasures and deals in the weekly estate auction every Thursday.
2613 Yates Avenue
Los Angeles, California 90040
323-724-8102
abell.com

Bonhams and Butterfields Auction House
7601 W. Sunset Boulevard
Los Angeles, California 90046
323-850-7500
bonhams.com

Castle Fabrics
Closeouts on designer fabric remnants for up to 80 percent off.
432 East 9th Street, # 3
Los Angeles, California 90015
213-612-0646

Council Thrift Shops
National Council of Jewish Women
Multiple locations in Los Angeles, California
323-651-2930
ncjwla.org

Long Beach Antique Flea Market
4901 East Conant Street
Long Beach, California 90808
323-655-5703
longbeachantiquemarket.com

Michael Levine Fabric
Amazing deals and huge selection located in the heart of the fabric district.
920 Maple Avenue
Los Angeles, California 90015
213-622-6259
mlfabric.com

Out of the Closet Thrift Stores
Locations in California and Florida
outofthecloset.org

Revivals Resale Mart
611 South Palm Canyon Drive
Palm Springs, California 92264
760-318-6491
revivalsresalemart.com

Rick Sanchez Moving and Restoration
Excellent repair and restoration of your finds. Pick-up and delivery.
310-980-6114
sanchezrulez@aol.com

Rose Bowl Flea Market
1001 Rose Bowl Drive
Pasadena, California 91103
323-560-7469
rosebowlstadium.com

Santa Monica Airport Outdoor Antique and Collectible Market
3050 Airport Avenue
Santa Monica, California 90405
323-933-2511
santamonicaairportantiquemarket.com

This Is Not Ikea
515 South Fairfax Avenue
Los Angeles, California 90036
323-938-9230
thisisnotikea.com

CONNECTICUT

Antique & Artisan Center
69 Jefferson Street
Stamford, Connecticut 06902
203-327-6022
antiqueandartisancenter.com

Braswell Galleries
1 Muller Avenue
Norwalk, Connecticut 06851
203-847-1234
braswellgalleries.com

Consigned Designs
115 Mason Street
Greenwich, Connecticut 06830
203-869-2165
consigneddesigns.com

Elephant's Trunk Flea Market
490 Danbury Road
New Milford, Connecticut 06776
860-355-1448
etflea.com

Elizabeth Jackson Estate Sales
Norwalk, Connecticut 06854
203-838-7636
ejacksonllc@msn.com
ejacksonllc.com

Greenwich Hospital Thrift Shop
199 Hamilton Avenue
Greenwich, Connecticut 06830
203-863-3933

Raphael's Furniture Restoration
Painting, repairing, restoring vintage furniture and fine antiques.
655 Atlantic Street
Stamford, Connecticut 06902
203-348-3079
raphaelsfurniture.com

Tiger Lily's
Upholstery, pillows, and accessories
154 Prospect Street
Greenwich, Connecticut 06830
203-629-6510

FLORIDA

Church Mouse
Run by the Episcopal Church of Bethesda by the Sea
378 South County Road
Palm Beach, Florida 33480
561-659-2154

Circa Who
Vintage finds, perfectly reinvented.
531 Northwood Road
West Palm Beach, Florida 33407
561-655-5224
circawho.com

Palm Beach Antiques & Design Center
6910 South Dixie Highway
West Palm Beach, Florida 33405
561-588-5868
palmbeachantique.com

SPARCC's Treasure Chest
Benefits victims of rape and domestic violence.
1426 Fruitville Road
Sarasota, Florida 34236
941-953-7800
sparcc.net/treasure.html

Woman's Exchange Thrift Shop
Supports the arts in Sarasota
539 South Orange Avenue
Sarasota, Florida 34236
941-955-7859
womansexchange.com

GEORGIA

Scott's Antique Markets
Atlanta Expo Center North
3650 Jonesboro Road
Atlanta, Georgia 30354
404-361-2000
scottantiquemarket.com

ILLINOIS

Brown Elephant Resale Shops
Multiple locations in Chicago, Illinois
howardbrown.org/
hb_brownelephant.asp

MASSACHUSETTS

Acushnet River Antiques Center
72 Kilburn Street
New Bedford, Massachusetts 02740
508-992-8878

Brimfield Antique and Flea Market Show
23 Main Street (Town Hall)
Brimfield, Massachusetts 01010
413-245-0030
brimfield.com

NEW HAMPSHIRE

Northeast Auctions
Great selection of antiques, and art at every price point
93 Pleasant Street
Portsmouth, New Hampshire 03801
603-433-8400
northeastauctions.com

NEW YORK

Antiques Garage Flea Market
112 West 25th Street
New York, New York 10001
212-243-5343
hellskitchenfleamarket.com

Brooklyn Flea
176 Lafayette Avenue
Brooklyn, New York 11238
718-935-1052
brooklynflea.com

Clarke Auction Gallery
2372 Boston Post Road
Larchmont, New York 10538
914-833-8336
clarkeny.com

Doyle New York Auction Gallery
175 East 87th Street
New York, New York 10128
212-427-2730
doylenewyork.com

Housing Works Thrift Stores
Benefits those living with AIDS
Multiple locations in New York
shophousingworks.com

Keno Auctions
127 East 69th Street
New York, New York 10021
212-734-2381
kenoauctions.com

Spence-Chapin Thrift Shop
Benefits children in need
1472 Third Avenue
New York, New York 10028
212-737-8448

Sotheby's Auction House
1334 York Avenue
New York, New York 10021
212-606-7000
sothebys.com

Tepper Galleries
110 East 25th Street
New York, New York 10010
212-677-5300
teppergalleries.com

TENNESSEE

World's Longest Yard Sale (every August)
675 miles from Michigan to Alabama along the 127 corridor
800-327-3945
127sale.com

TEXAS

Room Service Vintage
107 East North Loop Boulevard
Austin, Texas 78751
512-451-1057
roomservicevintage.com

Top Drawer Thrift Shop
4902 Burnet Road
Austin, Texas 78756
512-454-5161
topdrawerthrift.com

Treasure City
2142 East 7th Street
Austin, Texas 78702
512-524-2820
treasurecitythrift.org

WASHINGTON STATE

Seattle Antiques Market
1400 Alaskan Way
Seattle, Washington 98101
206-623-6115
seattleantiquesmarket.com

NATIONWIDE

Goodwill
800-741-0186
goodwill.org

Jonathan Adler Furniture and Accessories
jonathanadler.com

Salvation Army Thrift Shops
800-728-7825
salvationarmyusa.org

Society of Saint Vincent de Paul thrift stores
svdpusa.org

RESOURCES

estatesales.net
Find estate sales wherever you are in the United States.

lonnymag.com
If you miss *Domino* as much as I do, this is the website for you. Amazing interiors that embrace the mix of high and low.

etsy.com
An up-and-coming eBay alternative for handmade crafts and secondhand finds.

1stdibs.com
Pricey but fabulous selection of antique and vintage furnishings and art from dealers across the United States.

ebay.com
Twenty-four-hour online global yard sale. You name it, you can find it here.

Maine Antique Digest
Magazine with loads of information on antiques, restoration, and collecting. Great resource for auctions and antique shows across the country.
maineantiquedigest.com

Antiques and the Arts
Weekly newspaper serving collectors, and antique and arts community. Great information on antique shows, auctions, and estate sales.
antiquesandthearts.com

Davenport's Art Reference and Price Guide
Comprehensive index with data on more than 250,000 artists, including what their works sell for.

Acknowledgments

This book, a true work of passion and labor of love, would not have been possible without the help of the following people.

First, a big, fat kiss for my husband, David Haffenreffer, for holding down the fort while I was moonlighting as an author, designer, and junk hunter, and for allowing me to turn our house into an ever-evolving photo shoot and our garage into a storage unit worthy of an episode of *Hoarders*.

Thank you to photographer Michael McNamara, who went above and beyond the call of duty on our many hunting trips and shoots. You are a joy to work with and worked so hard to capture the essence of the insanity.

I also want to thank photographer Michael Williams, who discovered shooting a flea market is quite different than shooting a red carpet! And thank you to Cristopher Lapp for allowing me to use one of my favorite shots ever for my author photo.

Thank you to Rebecca DiLiberto for helping me harness my passion and organize the five thousand ideas I had into the various chapters and sections of this book. Your experience and style were invaluable.

Thank you to Kathy Griffin for trusting me with a huge job and allowing me to document it every step of the way. I know you were terrified by many of the "befores," but you had faith in my ability to find the beauty within, and encouraged me to follow my passion and trust my eye. You are the best friend and client a girl could ever ask for and I promise to never ask you to go to a yard sale again.

Thank you to Luis and Rick for helping me with the amazing transformations, and to Dervla Kelly and the team at Abrams for bringing it all together. I am honored to work with you. I am forever grateful to my agents, Andy McNicol and Jon Rosen, for enabling my addiction to rescuing, recycling, and reinventing other people's castoffs. Not many people knew I had this other life, and you believed I had something to share and encouraged me to follow my passion. Not to mention, you gave me the perfect excuse to go to yard sales and flea markets every weekend. It was research, after all!

And finally, thank you to my mom and dad. Mom, you taught me everything I know and I will forever cherish our Saturday morning hunts together. And Dad, who used to joke that my car always looked like *Sanford and Son*, filled to the brim with bric-a-brac, and yet got the biggest kick of all out of seeing what I did with "all that junk."

I wish you were here to see this book.

Published in 2011 by Stewart, Tabori & Chang
An imprint of ABRAMS

Text copyright © 2011 Lara Spencer
Illustrations copyright © 2011 Caitlin McGauley
Photographs copyright © 2011 Michael McNamara, www.shootingLA.com

Additional photography credits:
Pages 13 (top left), 38 (top and bottom right), 50 (middle left), 51 (bottom left, top and
bottom right), 78 (left), 79, 82 (left), 83 (left middle and bottom, right), 84, 85, 93 (right),
144 (right), 160 (left), 165 (bottom), copyright © 2012 Michael Williams
Pages 13 (bottom left), 121, copyright © by Jeff Dunn. Courtesy of *Antiques Roadshow*
Pages 14, 15 (right), 37 (bottom left), 64, 152, 169 (bottom left), copyright © 2012 Lara Spencer
Pages 16, 17, 22, 26, 29, 68, 117, 134, copyright © 2012 Aimee Herring
Page 20, copyright © 2012 Corbis
Page 105, copyright © 2012 Getty Images

Library of Congress Cataloging-in-Publication Data

Spencer, Lara.
I brake for yard sales / by Lara Spencer.
p. cm.
ISBN 978-1-58479-922-1 (alk. paper)
1. Shopping—Handbooks, manuals, etc. 2. Garage sales—Handbooks,
manuals, etc. I. Title.
TX335.S64 2011
381'.195—dc22
2011004182

Editor: Dervla Kelly
Designer: Alissa Faden
Production Manager: Tina Cameron

The text of this book was composed in Verlag, Bodoni, and FG Liz

Printed and bound in China
10 9 8 7 6 5 4 3 2 1

ABRAMS
THE ART OF BOOKS SINCE 1949
115 West 18th Street
New York, NY 10011
www.abramsbooks.com